TEXTILE TREASURES

NAOMI TARRANT

TEXTILE TREASURES

AN INTRODUCTION TO EUROPEAN DECORATIVE TEXTILES FOR HOME AND CHURCH IN THE NATIONAL MUSEUMS OF SCOTLAND

National Museums of Scotland Publishing Limited

Frontispiece:
*Detail from crewelwork
wall hanging, with the
'Tree of Life' pattern, dated
1719.
(A.1988.263A, see page 52)*

Cover:
*Detail from a large panel of
a knight slaying a dragon,
by Phoebe Anna Traquair,
dated 1904.
(A.1937.363, see page 72)*

Published by
NMS Publishing Limited
National Museums of Scotland
Chambers Street
Edinburgh EH1 1JF

© NMS Publishing Limited 2001

Text: © Naomi Tarrant and National Museums of Scotland 2001
Photographs: © Trustees of the National Museums of Scotland 2001

British Library Cataloguing in Publication Data
A catalogue record of this book
is available from the British Library.

ISBN 1 901663 64 7

Design by Elizabeth Robertson of NMS Publishing Limited.

Printed and bound by Craftprint International Ltd, Singapore.

CONTENTS

ACKNOWLEDGEMENTS

THE exhibition that inspired this publication was made possible by a very generous donation from Victoria Cairns, Lady of Finavon. This provided funding for a conservator to work on the pieces selected for exhibition. Without this donation it would not have been possible to show many of the items. Further gifts from two anonymous donors have also assisted towards this publication.

For help with various aspects of the writing of this book and compiling the entries on the embroideries, I particularly would like to thank Helen Bennett, formerly of the National Museum of Antiquities of Scotland, Clare Browne of the Victoria & Albert Museum, London, Mrs Elizabeth Burns, Elsa E Guðjónsson, Dr Bruce Lenman, Santina Levey, Julia Poole, Jennifer Scarce, Kay Staniland, Christine Stevens of the Museum of Welsh Folk Life, Cardiff, Patricia Wardle, and former and present colleagues in the National Museums of Scotland (NMS). Elizabeth Anne Haldane, as contract conservator, undertook the conservation work in NMS, together with Lynn McClean, Irene Kirkwood and Sarah Foskett of the Textile Conservation department. Thanks are also due to Leslie Florence and Joyce Smith, NMS photographers, who took the majority of the photographs. But, above all, the main thanks must go to the two people to whom this book is dedicated: Margaret Swain and Revel Oddy.

Opposite:
*An angel, Greek,
18th century — detail.*
(A.1946.62, see page 79)

MARGARET SWAIN, although always a freelance historian, has over the years since she came to Scotland in 1947, researched and published on the embroidery and textile heritage of the country and acted as advisor to the two museums — the Royal Scottish Museum and the National Museum of Antiquities of Scotland — whose collections are discussed in this book. She has been a dear friend to me since I came to Edinburgh and we have had many discussions on various embroidery topics over the years.

REVEL ODDY was the curator in charge of textiles, among all his other responsibilities, in the Royal Scottish Museum from 1955, and helped to build up the collections with some judicious acquisitions. He became Keeper in the Department of Art and Ethnography in 1974 when a full-time curator was appointed for the European costume and textiles. He was a wise mentor to his successor and I owe him a great debt for his help and encouragement.

Naomi Tarrant

INTRODUCTION

THIS book is not designed as a catalogue of an exhibition, but to provide the reader with an introduction to the collections of decorative household textiles of Europe in the National Museums of Scotland (NMS). The opportunity has also been taken to include the context of the founding collections that now make up NMS and to explain their growth and emphasis over the last two centuries.

The exhibition, 'Textile Treasures: Caring for a Collection' (November 2001) inspired the writing of this book. The event was a great opportunity to show some of the large embroidered hangings that NMS possesses and which, for various reasons, it is not always able to display. The centrepiece, and thus the main factor in determining what would be shown, are the wonderful wall hangings and accompanying valances dated 1719, which are almost certainly Scottish. Around these pieces, created in a form of needlework known as crewel-work, other items in the same technique were included to provide a context for the star items. The examples chosen are all dated from the early seventeenth century to the 1720s.

The selection of items for the exhibition, and for discussion in this book, is a personal one. As the first curator to be solely responsible for costume and textiles in the Royal Scottish Museum (later part of the National Museums of Scotland), I have had the pleasure of caring for this collection for over a quarter of a century. Some of the pieces chosen are great favourites, whilst others are recent acquisitions. They include the spectacular, such as the Kinghorne carpet, the unusual, such as the Icelandic hanging, and the rare, such as the Greek embroideries. Together they create some idea of the richness of European homes and public spaces, particularly in the seventeenth and early eighteenth centuries.

All enquiries concerning objects mentioned in this book, and requests for photographs, should specify the item's Accession number.

Naomi Tarrant

NATIONAL MUSEUMS OF SCOTLAND 2001

In the Heaven above

in the Earth beneath

in the Shelters under the Earth

COLLECTING POLICY

THE collecting philosophy of a museum is decided at its foundation. It may change or evolve over time as circumstances dictate, but this will not alter the formation of the original collection. A museum curator has to work with an existing collection and build on it, refining the collecting policy if necessary and perhaps extending its scope to take account of new areas or interests. Fashions in what are considered suitable for museums to collect change over time. The date limit for an antique, for example, was set at 1830. Anything after then was considered old or second-hand and certainly not worthy of being thought of as an antique. The interest in Victorian art began to appear in the 1950s, spearheaded by the Victoria & Albert Museum's exhibition of 1952, and this altered the perception of what was considered antique. Over the last few decades the distinction between antique, old or second-hand has disappeared.

There are also changes and developments in material culture. In the last quarter century the divisions between various types of art and craft have been challenged and broken. Today artists exist in most media, where before they may have been seen as craftspeople, and this is particularly true of textiles. In the past, textiles were produced as practical items for use in the home or to be fashioned into clothes. Today a textile may have no other use than as a picture for the wall, exactly like a painting. However, modern household textiles are generally seen as the preserve of industrial manufacturing, although this does not rule out design by an artist or designer. In part this change may be due to people today altering colour schemes in their homes, and moving house more often, usually making redecoration of a new abode part of the process.

A museum collection, if it is not to remain static, has to reflect these changes. However, there are dangers in collecting contemporary material virtually straight from the artist's studio. For example, there is no distance of time to judge a new style. Will it have staying power? Is it a flash in the pan? A passing phase that leaves no trace or influence in its wake? Will our successors regret a

Opposite:
*'Parable' by Lilian M Dring.
1941, an embroidered panel
for a bombed window.
given by the Needlework
Development Scheme.*
(A.1962.1059)

'Parable II' by Lilian M Dring, 1972-5, embroidered hanging, showing the use of plastic pill bubbles and other similar materials, the kind that might cause problems for conservation in the future. (K.1999.23)

particular acquisition and wish we had collected something else? Inevitably this will be the case because we cannot always be right in our selection. Another problem for any textile collection is the increased use of artificial fibres and plastics. These have an unknown shelf-life and the chemical composition of those currently in use are usually a trade secret, covered by patents, making it difficult for conservators to develop strategies for treating or storing them safely.[1] To accept some items as gifts may be permissible, but should public money, sometimes considerable sums, be spent on acquiring pieces? Already items of clothing from the 1960s and 1970s have had to be de-accessioned because they have deteriorated beyond a point where they can be conserved, and others are likely to experience a similar fate in the next few years.

Other criteria have become important in recent years. Museums were seen in the past as being apolitical, reflecting life but not shaping it. The educational role of the museum was to show the lifestyle of ancestors through their artefacts and the natural world, the development of the arts, or how technological change affected production. It might also act as an illustrated text book for designers, showing them the products of rival firms or the preferred taste that governed overseas markets. In the days before television the natural history collections illustrated the reality of the animal world, the true size of a lion or an elephant otherwise only seen in drawings. The crowded displays allowed both children and adults to look and wonder at the diversity and scale of a world they had little chance of experiencing themselves at first hand. As education has changed, and new sources of information have become available, the role of museums, what they collect and how they use those collections, has come under new pressures. Today museums are expected to deal with some of the current concerns of their audience while still remaining impartial. Whilst attempting to reflect the concerns of the school curricula, museums must also be places for the tourist and interested visitor. Through both permanent and temporary exhibitions, museums attempt to balance the different concerns and interest of their visitors.

How museum collections will be used in the future will depend on the use of new technologies. However, too great a reliance on seeing things in pictures on a computer screen and not in real life reduces us to the level of the Victorian audience who only knew a lion or a Turner painting from a drawing in a book. In an age when the pursuit of family history is growing, and is now probably the single most extensive leisure hobby, what our ancestors wore, made or used will become increasingly fascinating. Once past the bare branches of a genealogical tree, the family historian should be encouraged to seek the wider world of their ancestors. Museums should be an important step in their search. Access to museum collections has to be made easier if people are to see the real thing and to appreciate the wonders, not just of the natural world but of its man-made marvels.

At the present time the only way to show more of NMS's larger textiles is by including them in exhibitions like 'Textile Treasures'. In the future it is hoped that a new research centre will make them more widely accessible to those who are interested.

HOW A MUSEUM
COLLECTION
IS BUILT UP

AS well as money constraints, fashions in collecting and availability of material, the choice of items to add to a collection is influenced by the curator in charge and by the head of the museum. But the curator's personal decisions are probably the biggest influence on a collection. Curators work within their own background knowledge, interests and prejudices, but they are also influenced by what is in vogue and what is available. However, until a particular style or group of material becomes fashionable to collect, it can be difficult to find pieces. Also, until a certain length of time has passed, and the original owners of pieces die, there may be too few items available to make informed choices.

Private collectors usually concentrate on one type or style of material and can afford to be extremely persistent in tracking down pieces in unlikely places. A curator, on the other hand, has a full-time job that includes answering enquiries of greater or lesser complexity from the public, researching possible acquisitions, assisting colleagues, giving lectures or talks, sitting on various internal committees on anything from health and safety to temporary exhibitions, suggesting books for the library to purchase, reading relevant articles, and checking auction house catalogues. This is in addition to the basic care of existing collections and making them available to visitors and researchers. Curators in a national museum also have a remit outside their own institution, to provide help on request to colleagues in other museums, or to offer advice to other bodies, such as the Heritage Lottery Fund, the National Art Collections Fund, or the National Fund for Acquisitions which helps the non-national museums with money for purchases. This does not allow for the single-minded pursuit by a collector of their chosen interest.

Nor is it considered ethical for a curator to have a personal collection within the field that they care for in the museum, and to a certain extent a curator's collecting instinct, or 'squirrel mentality' as some unkindly refer to it, is satisfied by the collection they curate. Although it is not a curator's personal collection and they

Opposite:
*Peacock – detail
from crewelwork cover
with shepherd and
shepherdess, c. 1700.
(A. 1949. 224, see page 59)*

5

will have to relinquish control of it some day, there is great satisfaction in acquiring items.

Where the acquisitions come from depends on the type of collection. Trawling through jumble and car boot sales, antique markets and second-hand shops might produce the odd item, but it is not necessarily a productive use of a curator's time. For some items the specialist dealer has been a great source of information and help in acquiring pieces to fill particular gaps or, on a more practical level, bidding at auction. Auctions on the Internet are now common, so adding to collections is becoming more complicated. Today the pressure of the job means that bureaucracy, accountability and financial restraints all impose their own timetables. In a large collection too, what the museum needs and what it can afford in both money and space, is also limited.

The traditional methods of building up a collection are through gift, bequest and purchase. There are one or two other sources, such as exchange of items with another institution, but these do not usually account for more than a very small proportion of a museum's collection. For archaeological or ethnographical items, excavation and fieldwork are important sources. How donors decide on where to place their gifts depends on what the items are and where the person lives. Although the National Museums of Scotland covers the whole of the country, there are many donors who would prefer to give to their local institution. This has implications for pieces that are seen to be of national importance. Should they go to Edinburgh or should they be held in the locality? There are strong arguments on both sides, and at different times one or other gains the strongest support.

In the past, collectors often left their collections to their home city or town as the foundation of a new museum. Today's collectors often dislike museums because they feel pieces are lost forever to them, and that eventually there will be nothing left for new enthusiasts to acquire. Thus their accumulated treasures are usually sold at auction so that others can have the fun of acquiring pieces. However, unless a good catalogue is produced, all the information that has been built up on their particular area of interest can be lost. Another problem can arise if the new owner is not interested in all the documentation, particularly provenance, *ie* information on where an item may have originated from. This vital information may equally well have been withheld when the piece was sold.

When the two national museums based in Edinburgh – the National Museum of Antiquities of Scotland and the Royal Scottish Museum – amalgamated in 1985, the pattern of their collecting of textiles showed many similarities.

The National Museum of Antiquities of Scotland originated as the Society of Antiquaries of Scotland, founded in 1780. Its main area of interest was the archaeological antiquities that were starting to be unearthed, which attracted much attention during this period. When objects began to be given to the Society and a museum started, the objects collected ranged far wider than Scotland, including material from Egypt and the Pacific.

In 1780 there were few models for museums and the Society followed broadly the same wide scope of the British Museum, including the natural world.[2] For the Society the cost of running the museum soon became a problem, and in the mid-nineteenth century it applied to the government for help. In return for funding the collection, the Society had to make it over in perpetuity for the free use and admission of the public. The first printed catalogue of the collection, produced in 1892, shows several items of clothing or personal possessions but no domestic textiles. The first non-clothing textiles acquired were a mort cloth in 1905, and a sixteenth-century embroidered chalice veil bought in 1919.

The Royal Scottish Museum, originally known as the Industrial Museum, was founded in 1854 and funded from the profits of the Great Exhibition of 1851. These had been set aside to provide for institutions of learning that included the Victoria & Albert Museum in London. The Industrial Museum was intended to be a museum of industry of the world with special relation to Scotland.[3] As well as exhibition galleries, it was to have a laboratory for the testing and the analysis of materials, a workshop for investigating industrial apparatus, a library and a lecture theatre. The new museum lacked a building and land was purchased. In 1864 the first part of the museum's new home was occupied and the name changed to the Edinburgh Museum of Science and Art. By 1875 the original planned building was complete and the museum was divided into various sections including Constructive Art, Food, Agriculture and Medicine, Natural History, Minerals, Raw Materials, Manufactures, and Applied Chemistry. In 1904, on its fiftieth anniversary, the name was changed yet again to the Royal

Central motif on a bed quilt showing the oriental figures, early 18th century, given by the Needlework Development Scheme. (A.1962.1055)

Scottish Museum. By then the museum was seen as housing a systematic, comparative and chronological series desired by an educational establishment.

In effect, part of the museum's remit was to collect contemporary industrial production and older or foreign pieces showing examples of good design. The aim was to help British manufacturers make products for export that were suitable for their markets, and to show what their rivals elsewhere in the world were producing. For manufacturers, in an age before well-illustrated cheap books, and when few could afford to travel far for pleasure or 'research', having examples within a train ride in their own country was seen as an enormous benefit.

The first textiles that entered this museum illustrated the process from raw material to finished product, for example from the cotton boll to the printed fabric. But the real collecting of textiles as historical items only started later in both institutions. The National Museum of Antiquities of Scotland concentrated on Scottish fabrics, such as blankets and tartan samples, showing mostly hand production; whilst the Royal Scottish Museum, in keeping with its original foundation, collected textiles from around the world with both an aesthetic and technical interest. On the whole the Royal Scottish Museum appears to have collected the higher status pieces – including some Scottish items such as the Lochleven hanging in 1921, then thought to be the work of Mary, Queen of Scots, and later the Linlithgow hanging which has a similar history. However, by the 1970s more interest was being shown by the National Museum of Antiquities of Scotland in acquiring these higher status items, and various decorative household textiles were acquired from 1973 onwards[4], including the spectacular Kinghorne carpet. There had also been a transfer of items between the two museums, such as the Egyptian and ethnographic pieces to the Royal Scottish Museum, and the tartan and Fair Isle pieces to the National Museum of Antiquities of Scotland. These were items that were seen as more relevant to the other museum's collection. The remit of the two establishments had therefore been complementary since the beginning, and the amalgamation in 1985 was a means of making this more concrete.

When the two museums were amalgamated, the official motto, adapted in 1985, was 'Presenting Scotland to the World and the World to Scotland'. This was originally coined by George Wilson, the first director of the Industrial Museum in 1858, and it effectively described what was happening at that time. The collecting policy of NMS today is governed by the following criteria – national importance and the potential for display, education and research. Subsidiary to these objectives are whether items are of significance in relation to their discipline, or whether they fill gaps in a collection or illuminate interesting holdings in the museum and elsewhere (eg regional diversity).

Among the earliest and most interesting foreign pieces to be accepted by the Royal Scottish Museum were two fragments of embroidered hangings which were allegedly used in the tent that housed the Althing, the Icelandic Parliament. These came to the museum in 1858. Icelandic embroidery is fairly rare and these pieces are important items in the collection. But they were not the only Icelandic examples the museum acquired, as several items of clothing were also bought. This emphasises the close links between Scotland and northern Europe, which have existed for many centuries.

Over the years the greatest numbers of foreign embroideries that have entered the museum have originated from Greece. This represents an interest in this work by British people, particularly classical archaeologists working in Greece, such as Theodore Bent, Robert Bosanquet, whose collection is now in Tyne and Wear Museum, and Richard Dawkins and Alan Wace, who both gave pieces to the Victoria & Albert Museum.[5] Other major collections in Britain include the National Museums and Galleries on Merseyside, and the Whitworth Art Gallery in Manchester.

The NMS's collection of about fifty pieces is not large in comparison with some of the other collections mentioned, but it does include two wonderful long embroideries that are probably altar frontals and rather rare.

Each of these two embroidery traditions is very different to the ones we are more used to seeing in Britain, but both are within the traditions of European work as it has evolved over the centuries. They add an interesting contrast to the needle-work that is mainly from the British Isles, and are in keeping with the earlier ethos of the Royal Scottish Museum of showing the industries and crafts of other countries. However, by 1900 the museum's former emphasis had changed and in one respect it had become much more a museum of decorative arts. This led in the first half of the twentieth century to the acquisition of older pieces rather than contemporary material, and several large embroidered curtains, hangings and bed covers were collected. The museum could not afford some of the really spectacular items that private collectors, like Sir William Burrell or Sir Frederick Richmond, were able to purchase, although items from the latter's collection have been acquired by the museum at later dates.

Occasionally sets of hangings were split between the Royal Scottish and the Victoria & Albert or other museums, which spread the burden of cost. The rationale for splitting sets was that the individual pieces were perceived as representing a form of embroidery, or a particular design. By having at least a single example, the development of style could be shown. Additionally, before the advent of good illustrated catalogues, this splitting up of identical embroideries was seen as a better way of showing material to the widest number of people. However, this has meant that the effect of a full set when displayed in a room is lost, and therefore the acquisition by the National Museums of Scotland in 1988 of the 1719 set, described on pages 53-7, is very important to our understanding of how such rooms would have appeared.

The largest collection of items donated to the NMS's costume and textile section, that of Charles Stewart of Shambellie, given in 1977, consists almost entirely of costume. Although gifts are important to the textile collections, many of the larger pieces described in this book have been bought at auction, from a dealer, or very occasionally from a private individual. One particularly large collection – that of Sir Joseph Noel Paton – was acquired in 1905. This consisted mainly of arms and armour; it also included some textiles. More recently, examples of the fabrics designed by the American, Jack Lenor Larsen, were added. Their acquisition came about because of one curator's personal acquaintance with the designer, which enabled the museum to acquire examples no longer in production, and therefore to cover a wider date range. But the largest number of items in the collection which have been bought have come from dealers, and in the last fifty years one of the principal sources has been the firm of Arditti and Mayorcas, later Mayorcas, in London. The growth of textile sales by the main auction houses has, since the mid-1970s, also been a source for the acquisition of items.

Furnishing fabric of silk and polyester, hand woven with stripes and hand printed with a large dahlia design. 'Dahlias on Siamese brocade', Jack Lenor Larsen design, made in Thailand, 1972. (A.1979.228)

NATIONAL ART COLLECTIONS FUND

Museums have rarely had generous grants for purchasing pieces, so other sources of income have had to be sought. One of the earliest, and most generous, has been the National Art Collections Fund, which for nearly a hundred years has been using the money raised from its members to help all kinds of museums, and other public bodies, acquire important works of art. The first textile item it helped the Royal Scottish Museum to purchase was the panel of the Lochleven wall hangings in 1921. At the time these were thought to have been worked by Mary, Queen of Scots, but they are now known to have been created in a professional embroidery workshop, probably in Edinburgh. However the 1719 hangings, which form the centrepiece of the exhibition, and the Kinghorne carpet, are the two most outstanding textiles to receive assistance for their purchase. Sometimes donors give pieces to the Fund to be distributed to specific museums, and the National Museums of Scotland has benefited from this. More recently the Heritage Lottery Fund has also helped numerous purchases by NMS, but none so far of textiles.

*Detail of 'Parable' by
Lilian M Dring, 1941.
(A.1962.1059, see page x)*

*Three dimensional tapestry
made as a small parcel by
Archie Brennan, 1974, given
by the Scottish Arts Council.
(K.1997.1112)*

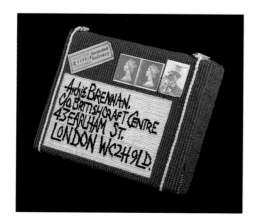

NEEDLEWORK DEVELOPMENT SCHEME

Other large donations have consisted of collections rather than money. In 1961 the Needlework Development Scheme was disbanded and its collection of over 3500 historic and contemporary needlework was dispersed to various museums and art colleges in Britain. The Scheme was formed in 1934 to encourage a greater interest in embroidery and to raise the standard of design. Its intention was to establish a collection of embroidery, from Britain and other countries, to which various institutions, such as schools and colleges, would have access. By 1960 there were 158 collections in circulation. Several exhibitions and publications were also produced. Central to the Scheme was an expert who was replaced at regular intervals to ensure a consistently fresh approach. This helped to make the collection of embroideries a good source of contemporary European work.

When the Scheme's collection was dispersed, the Royal Scottish Museum acquired 213 pieces of embroidery from the 1920s to late 1950s period, created by embroiderers all over Britain and Europe. The majority of the items were mid-twentieth century European household textiles. An exhibition showing this magnificent gift was held in 1965 and a catalogue produced.[6]

SCOTTISH DEVELOPMENT AGENCY AND SCOTTISH ARTS COUNCIL

More recently, the collections of the Scottish Development Agency and the Scottish Arts Council have been dispersed. The former had built up a collection of contemporary Scottish crafts between 1979 and 1989, and this had been sent round the country to different venues as a showcase for the crafts.[7] When the Agency was disbanded, the collection in its entirety was given to NMS. As well as textiles there was glass, ceramics, jewellery, metalwork and furniture. The Scottish Arts Council's collection, on the other hand, consisted mainly of paintings and prints, with some tapestries and ceramics. NMS acquired five large tapestries and two smaller pieces from this collection, including the witty Archie Brennan tapestry 'parcel', complete with a real stamp, that was sent through the post for an exhibition in London.

With the Agency's collection NMS had no choice in the items it received because it accepted the complete collection built up by a committee of crafts people. It is of interest nonetheless, because the collection reflects a decade of Scottish craft-work at a time of change.

Collecting contemporary work poses problems because it is impossible to know which maker will continue to be relevant to their craft in ten or twenty years from now. The Agency's collection is therefore invaluable as it represents a snapshot in time and was created using the judgement of the peer group of craftspeople.

The Scottish Arts Council had a much larger collection brought together over a longer period of time. Museums from all over Scotland were invited to bid for items and to explain why they wanted to acquire them. For a large collection, like the one NMS already holds, the criteria for choosing had to be carefully thought out. Whilst it did not get all the items it would have liked, the museum did acquire a range of work that helped to fill gaps, including two pieces that were items NMS had wanted to acquire several years previously. In the past the Scottish Arts Council had first choice of the work when they supported a craft or art exhibition, so NMS was not able to acquire them.

Tapestry by Veronica Togneri, 'Colonsay and Oransay, early Spring 1981', given by the Scottish Development Agency. (A.1991.172)

DECORATIVE
HOUSEHOLD TEXTILES

TEXTILES used in the home, or in public spaces, were opportunities for decoration that gave colour to any interior as well as adding a feeling of warmth. There is a long-standing tradition for the use of textiles in this way, examples having been recorded in the graves from the Altai region of Siberia of the mid-first millennium BC, and from the tomb of Tutankhamun (early 14th century BC) in Egypt. In Northern Europe, the Bayeaux 'Tapestry' of the late eleventh century is an example of what was obviously a long-established tradition of decorative household textiles. During the mediaeval period, embroideries, painted and stamped cloths and woven tapestries all found favour as a means to brighten and warm up a room. In wealthy households, textiles were transported from castle to castle as owners moved around their estates, as individual land holdings were often separated by quite long distances. Textiles were easier to transport than furniture and it was cheaper than having a separate set for each building. However, they were vulnerable to decay from moths, water, misuse or disaster whilst being transported.

Changing fashions in house layout also meant that textiles might be cut up to fit a new space, and when no longer good enough for main rooms they could be relegated to the rooms of servants, or stored away, forgotten about, in some attic. By the sixteenth century King Henry VIII of England, for example, kept his various palaces and castles furnished, and the inventory of possessions taken at his death in 1547 reveals how sumptuous some of his rooms must have been with all the textiles he had acquired.[8] Something of the richness of furnishings in a late sixteenth-century house can still be seen at Hardwick Hall, Derbyshire, the home built and furnished by the redoubtable Bess of Hardwick.[9] In her will, Bess decreed that none of the furnishings should be sold or given away, and although time and decay have inevitably meant some losses, there is still enough left to show how magnificently the house was furnished around 1600.

The NMS collection of decorative household textiles does not contain any examples earlier than the sixteenth century, because this kind of material has not

Opposite:
European bison – detail
from a tapestry fragment,
16th century.
(A.1956.1439, see page 17)

survived well above ground. Examples of fragments that may well be household textiles, such as blankets, have been found in excavations of mediaeval sites, but it depends on conditions being right for the preservation of such material. In the past, when all fabric was made by hand, it was expensive to produce and people tended to reuse it until it was no longer fit for anything but rags. Cutting-up and remaking were, therefore, particular hazards for fabrics, and this is something that still goes on. For example, many tapestries showing patches of wear have the good parts cut out and made into cushion covers.

The types of textiles that are in NMS's collections include tapestries, embroidered wall and bed hangings and valances, cushions, fire screens, upholstered furniture, lengths of furnishing silks and printed cottons, and many small embroidered pictures from the raised work of the seventeenth century to the Berlin wool work of the nineteenth.

TAPESTRY

The most costly wall hangings were those made of tapestry, a woven technique which produces strong, durable hangings capable of taking a complicated and colourful design. These were made in workshops by professionally-trained weavers, the most famous workshops being in the Low Countries, *ie* modern Belgium and the Netherlands, or northern France. The tapestries were often woven in sets of five, seven or more panels, in wool on wool or linen warps, and they were originally commissioned by wealthy patrons. After a design had been woven once, it could be repeated to a different size, or with additions such as a coat of arms. Historical subjects, biblical tales, or stories from myths and classical literature were all popular themes, and the subject chosen might represent a particularly apposite one for the occasion, such as a marriage, that prompted the commission. Today these tapestries can cause confusion because the designers chose to represent the people in the tapestry in contemporary clothes, so that the biblical marriage of Jacob (Genesis 29), for example, might be depicted as the marriage of a sixteenth-century king and queen. The stories on the tapestries were the secular equivalent of the frescos and paintings that adorned churches. They were stories for the edification, enlightenment and enjoyment of the owner, his friends and visitors, who, even if they were illiterate, would have understood the stories from the classics, myths and history. Some tapestries, on the other hand, were merely decorative and illustrated with plants, for example; or personal and decorated with heraldic motifs. Because of their robustness many late mediaeval tapestries survive today, including the 'Lady and the Unicorn' series in the Museé du Moyen Age in Paris, and the Devonshire Hunting tapestries in the Victoria & Albert Museum.

NMS's earliest tapestry is a panel from a series of the Virtues. It shows Prudence riding in a chariot surrounded by people from history and mythology who exemplified the virtue of prudence (Accession number A.1898.324). Woven in the Low Countries about 1530, it was bought in 1898 from the Eudel sale in Paris. Like many tapestries it was mutilated at a later date, suffering the loss of its top border which was replaced by a painted strip, and its blue outer guard border replaced in the 1970s.

An interesting fragment in the collection is probably from a tapestry showing an animal park, a popular theme in the sixteenth century (Accession number A.1956.1439). What makes this piece of particular interest is the depiction of the rare European bison, with a face of a rather benign lion (by this date the European bison was confined to Poland); and the presence of the also rare 'Dragon's Blood Tree', *Dracaena draco*, amidst other more common forest trees and animals. The Dragon's Blood Tree originated in the Canary Islands and was noted for its red resin. Possible pictorial sources for both of these unusual species are the German woodcuts and engravings of the earlier part of the sixteenth century. For example, both Martin Schongauer in 1470 and Albrecht Dürer in 1504 reproduced the tree in their engravings of the Holy Family's Flight into Egypt (Matthew 2:19-21). Only one further example from the same design is known. This is from a photograph that shows an almost complete tapestry with a unicorn in the centre.[10]

A seventeenth-century panel from the 'Decius Mus' series illustrates the exploits of the Roman general of that name (Accession number A.1905.1017). The NMS panel is the first in the set, showing Decius Mus telling his troops of his resolution to die in the forthcoming battle. The story can be found in Livy, book VIII. The cartoons, *ie* the original drawings from which the tapestry was woven, were drawn by Peter Paul Rubens and are now in the Liechtenstein collection. In the border, still intact, there are the weavers' mark for Jan Raes I's workshop, the city mark

Tapestry fragment showing a European bison and a Dragon's Blood tree, Flemish, 16th century. (A.1956.1439)

Furnishing silk, red satin ground with damask design of small flowers, fruit and leaves and a brocaded design in gilt metal of exotic flowers and coronets, Italian, c. 1640. (A.1984.55)

of a shield, and 'BB' which stands for Brussels. It was a popular series as several sets exist, but the museum's panel would appear to have been woven from the original cartoon, not too long after the first commissioned set was made in 1617.

This tapestry was in Sir Joseph Noel Paton's collection, but there are no records of where he acquired it. Paton used objects from his collection in many of his paintings, including a tapestry showing 'David and Abigail' (1 Samuel 25) (Accession number A.1905.1019). It can be seen in the background to the painting created in 1866, now in a private collection, 'I wonder who lived in there?', which shows Noel Paton's son looking into a mediaeval helmet.

The collection has been brought up to date by NMS with purchases from the Edinburgh Tapestry Company, founded in 1912 by the Marquis of Bute with weavers from Merton Abbey, the workshop founded by William Morris.[11] The company wove the very large tapestry, 'Corryvechan', located in the entrance to the new Museum of Scotland building. The tapestry was designed by Kate Whiteford especially for this space (Accession number K.1998.1794).

Today the term 'tapestry' covers many processes, materials and ways of producing wall hangings, which do not necessarily include the traditional techniques of tapestry weaving. There are also many individual artists who weave tapestries or make wall hangings, and examples of their work are represented in the NMS collection. The city of Edinburgh has been at the centre of this renaissance in tapestry since the 1960s because of the work of the tapestry department in the Edinburgh College of Art. Other initiatives, such as The Weavers' Workshop that Revel Oddy was instrumental in establishing in the early 1970s, have also helped, providing areas for work and display at a time when commercial galleries were not interested and other gallery space was limited in the city.[12]

FABRICS

Other forms of household textiles produced by professionally-trained workers are the woven and printed fabrics. Fabric, as wall coverings, became more general in the eighteenth century, and the same material was often used to cover chairs and settees, as well as the window curtains, giving unity to the room decoration. Silk damask was a particular favourite, but other weaves such as brocade and cut velvet were also popular.

Furnishing satin, showing a large tree, with bird and a castle in the background, the design produced by the ikat technique, 1839. (A.1982.2)

NMS has many types of furnishing fabrics in its collections. Originally only small pieces were collected, but more recently attempts have been made to acquire larger lengths so that the full effect of the fabric when hung can be appreciated. These include some examples of seventeenth-century Italian furnishing silks with fairly bold patterns. Furnishing silks often have linen included to strengthen the fabric.

Among some of the more unusual examples is one woven in linen with extra coloured wool wefts imitating a flame or Irish stitch pattern (Accession number A.1962.500). This was probably woven at Elbeuf in France in the early eighteenth century. Another notable piece is made of satin with a printed warp ikat design of a large tree with landscape. It came with a note: 'One of the curtains used on board the Emperor of Russia's yatch [*sic*] purchased by My Mother at Howell & James 1839' (Accession number A.1982.2). Howell and James were silk mercers in Regent Street, London, and Nicholas I was the Emperor of Russia at that time. Lady Charlotte Guest saw his steam yacht being built at Fairbairn's yard, Millwall, and later witnessed its launch in May 1838.[13] The silk is particularly wide –

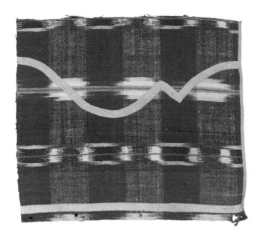

Fustian (cotton and linen),
ikat, French, from the
Charente region,
19th century.
(A.1983.1203)

Printed furnishing cotton,
French, by Favre Petitpierre
et Cie of Nantes, about
1820. Printed with four
scenes from 'The Lady of
the Lake' by Sir Walter
Scott, 1810, a popular
author whose stories
provided inspiration for
many artists and craftsmen
throughout Europe at this
period.
(A.1978.401)

1125mm – and 1105mm long, with the top of the design missing. It is not clear if this was an actual panel used on the yacht, or part of the fabric that was left over.

By the mid-eighteenth century, printed cotton and linen produced in Britain became popular for furnishing fabrics. These were cheaper than Indian painted cottons, and supply was probably more reliable as the latter depended upon whatever ships' captains could obtain and the uncertainties of the voyage back to Britain. Among the many examples of printed furnishing cotton in the NMS collection are examples from the French printing works at Jouy and Nantes, as well as pieces of provincial French blue ikats. Again these vary from small fragments to longer lengths.

Recently NMS has acquired two cotton curtains and a valance, dating from *c.*1785-95 (Accession number K.2000.436). The cotton, which is quite coarsely woven, has faint blue threads down the selvages. This indicates the fabric was woven in Britain between the years 1774-1811, when all home-manufactured

Printed furnishing cotton,
English, c. 1785-95,
showing Diana and her
attendants shooting
at a live tethered bird.
(K.2000.436)

cotton had by law to carry this distinguishing feature. The design is printed in sepia by the plate print process, in which the cotton was printed using engraved copper plates in the same way an engraving on paper was made. The two scenes incorporated into the design are from different sources and show Apollo in one and Diana in the other. The latter scene is taken from the engraving of a painting by Domenichino in the Borghese Gallery, Rome (dated 1617-18). It is an almost exact pictorial representation of a passage from Virgil's *Aeneid* (Book V, lines 485-518) which describes the shooting at a live bird which is tethered.

LINEN DAMASK

Another decorative household textile that became important during the sixteenth century was white figured linen damask for tablecloths, napkins and towels. Tablecloths and napkins made of this material added elegance to a table. The way the linen was laundered accentuated the contrasts in the two weaves used to make damask, and this feature, when it caught the light, gave a richness and depth to the fabric. In a dining room, table linen played an important part in the furnishing of the room when in use.

Household inventories often listed massive quantities of table linen. Sometimes in Scotland the table appeared better provided for with linen than the bed. Most of the table linen was made up of small patterned damask, woven with repeating geometric motifs. However, the most expensive was the figured damask, where the linen was woven with biblical, classical or historical events, or with floral motifs, the design repeating in the length and across the width. Other popular motifs included heraldic, war and hunting scenes, as well as commemorative designs celebrating some victory, or a dynastic marriage.

The best linen damask was produced in the Low Countries. Large suites of it were ordered by both royal and noble households from the main centres of damask production, particularly for major events. A royal marriage or coronation, with the attendant feasts, would require huge quantities of linen. If the required amount could not be supplied in full from existing stocks, new linen would have to be ordered. By the mid-seventeenth century Scottish weavers were attempting to weave damask, but it was not until 1700 that definite Scottish examples can be identified. From 1700 until nearly the end of the century, the NMS collection contains a series of napkins, and later tablecloths, that show the names of the couple who had commissioned the weaving of the pieces and a date. In comparison with the damask from the Low Countries, the designs are often rather crude and the weaving is technically not as competent, but it shows how widespread the use of good table linen had become. Quite where all the eighteenth-century damasks were woven in Scotland is not known, but two napkins survive in the collection with the place of manufacture woven in the piece – Edinburgh and Hamilton.[14]

The NMS collection includes a large group of Scottish damasks as well as examples from other countries. One of the most important is the example by Passchier Lammertin of the Royal Arms of England, woven *c.* 1603 (Accession number A.1970.1194). An earlier example is one with a portrait of Queen Elizabeth I and her coat of arms, also woven in Flanders (Accession number A.1962.1015). There are also several large tablecloths showing various biblical scenes, including one depicting the story of Susannah and the Elders (*The Apocrypha*, 'The History of Susannah' in Joshua 2), probably woven at Courtrai in the seventeenth century to an earlier design (Accession number K.1999.572). The story of Joshua and the Spies (Joshua 2) is shown on another Flemish piece (Accession number H.SN8),

and there are also many napkins, including a set of six, each woven with part of a design of the story of Tobias and the Angel (*The Apocrypha*, Tobit 5-13) (Accession number K.1999.573).

CARPETS

Carpets were brought into Europe from the East – Turkey and Persia – where the art of carpet-weaving, by knotting short lengths of wool or silk round a warp and weft of a coarser fibre, such as wool, linen or hemp, had achieved great artistry by the end of the fifteenth century. Examples of these eastern carpets can be seen in many of the paintings of the period, and in the portrait by Hans Holbein of Henry VIII of England in the 1530s. Many of these carpets came into Europe as diplomatic gifts, but examples of carpets commissioned by Europeans in the east are recorded

24

and some still exist. The making of carpets in Britain is found in documents from as early as the 1520s when the second Earl of Ormonde and Ossory established a workshop in Kilkenny, Ireland for making 'tapestry, diaper, Turkey carpets, cushions *etc*' using weavers from Flanders.[15] This is an interesting mixture of techniques as 'tapestry' and 'diaper', a term usually describing a form of white linen damask, are two very different forms of weaving, whilst the carpets, and possibly the cushions, are knotted. Certainly these were all areas where the Flemish weavers are known to have been skilled. The accounts show that the earl was keen to improve his household furnishings as well as invest in an area that his neighbours and peers would also be interested in, *ie* the acquisition of luxury goods for their new homes. The inventories of Henry VIII show what the king had acquired and inherited, but the splendour of his court must also have encouraged his nobles to emulate him, even if they could not compete in scale.

The Earl of Ormonde's Kilkenny workshop probably indicates the type of small estate-run business that may have produced most of the surviving carpets attributed to manufacture within the British Isles. The lifetime of the business was probably short, but perhaps its Flemish weavers were able to move from one workshop to another, taking their skills with them. There are only twelve sixteenth and seventeenth-century carpets of British manufacture known to survive and NMS is fortunate to own one of them. This is the carpet found at Glamis Castle, Forfar, the home of the earls of Strathmore and Kinghorne. It was bought in 1980 with a generous donation from the National Art Collections Fund.

The Kinghorne carpet, as it is now known, is a long rectangular carpet of a red-ground Indo-Persian design with a symmetrical knot (Accession number H.SO20).[16] The central panel is composed of vine scrolls and palmettes, with a wide border of alternating circular and rectangular cartouches, filled with more scrolls and flowers. The narrow borders separating the wider border from the central panel and also the outer border are, however, copied from the European needlework tradition, with carnation scrolls between twisted guilloche borders. At one short end is a crowned monogram with the letters 'M', 'E', 'I', 'L', 'C' and 'K'.

Analysis of the dyes used has been carried out using ultraviolet visible spectro-photometry and thin layer chromatography. The basic dye stuffs were identified

Opposite:
*Kinghorne carpet,
English,* c. *1620.*
(*H.SO 20*)

*Detail of the monogram
on the Kinghorne carpet.
(H.SO 20, see page 24)*

as indigotin for the blues, madder and old fustic in the orange, kermes in the red-brown, and an unknown tannin dye for the black-brown. The red ground is cochineal from South America, which helps to confirm the European origin for the carpet as lac would have been the dye used in the east. Fortunately the yellows were in good condition and analysis revealed luteolin and genistein, the main colouring components of dyer's greenwood. This was a common dye source before *c.*1671, but very rare after this date. It was common in central and southern Europe and most areas of England, but not in the rest of the British Isles. Greens were produced from indigotin and dyer's greenwood by over-dyeing. The dye analysis therefore suggests that the carpet was made in Europe, between *c.*1530 when South American dyes began to be used in Europe and *c.*1670 when dyer's greenwood fell out of use.[17]

The Kinghorne carpet was found at Glamis Castle in the late 1970s, in use on the floor. It had been discovered by the then Countess of Strathmore, although it was not realised at first how old or indeed how rare it was. The history of the carpet is unknown as no bills or other documentation have so far been found, although it is possible that in the inventory of 1648 it is one of the 'tu greyt carpets and a lesser one' which are mentioned. A later inventory (1712) lists in the Great Hall 'four oak tables al covered with a fine large carpet ... a large oak table covered with a carpet'.[18] The monogram on the carpet is also found in the plaster ceiling of the room known as King Malcolm's Room, which dates from 1620. It should probably be read as 'John Lyon, Comes [Earl] of Kinghorne and Margaret Erskine'. Margaret was a daughter of the Earl of Mar and John Lyon's first wife. They were married in 1618. About 1640 John married Lady Elizabeth Maule, his second wife, so the initials could equally belong to her.

John Lyon's father, Patrick, had been one of the Scottish nobles who went south with James VI of Scotland when he inherited the English throne in 1603. Patrick received many favours from the king, including his earldom in 1606. Although he started to improve and extend Glamis Castle, it was his son John who had the elaborate plaster ceilings made.[19] He used English plasterers, who also made similar ceilings at Muchalls and Craigievar, and it is possible that he also engaged carpet weavers at Glamis to make him one or more carpets. Alternatively John may have ordered them to be made in London. The suggestion that the monogram stands for 'Margaret Erskine' rather than 'Elizabeth Maule' is therefore strengthened, when the extension and decoration of Glamis in the early 1620s is taken into account. Margaret Erskine, who was a fervent Presbyterian and a supporter of the Covenanting cause, pushed her husband into supporting the Covenanters against Charles I which drained the estate financially. The deprivations continued with Elizabeth Maule's second husband, the Earl of Linlithgow, who cruelly treated his stepson and wasted the estates further.

When Patrick, the third Earl of Kinghorne and later first Earl of Strathmore (1643-1695), took control of his inheritance in 1660 and started to live at Glamis, he found the castle denuded of furniture and furnishings and virtually derelict. It took him ten years before he could repair the castle because of the state it was in, and the state of his finances. He bought back some of the furniture from his stepfather, but there is no record of the carpet.[20] During the eighteenth century more building work and the death of several earls in quick succession left Glamis uninhabited by the family for many years, and it is not clear where the carpet might have been during this period.[21] It certainly does not appear to have been used in the castle during the nineteenth or early twentieth centuries.

Detail of a Scotch carpet, 19th century.
(H.SO 21)

The good condition of the Kinghorne carpet today suggests it was used mainly as a table cover and not on the floor until its recent discovery. This illustrates the fact that these spectacular carpets were so rare and expensive that they were used for show. Having them on the floor was an option for only the really wealthy and flamboyant.

Carpets became much more general during the eighteenth century and were often included in a room's decorative scheme. On the whole NMS does not have many European carpets, although it has a large collection of Middle Eastern examples and has added more from contemporary workshops making carpets in this tradition from Romania. A mid twentieth-century carpet in the collection was designed by Frank Brangwyn and made by the carpet firm of Templeton's of Glasgow (Accession number A.1981.167). Its design was only woven to commission and five examples are known to have been made. The NMS carpet was originally made for the seller's parents in 1933.

More homely examples were the so-called 'Scotch' or ingrain carpets, woven on a loom with a reversible design so that each side could be used. Examples survive from the nineteenth century, although the place of manufacture is not always known. NMS has several examples.[22]

THE DOMESTIC
EMBROIDERER

LEARNING HOW TO EMBROIDER

By the far the largest number of surviving decorative household textiles in the NMS collection are embroidered.

Domestic embroidery in Britain is only really known from the mid-sixteenth century, when examples begin to survive. Mediaeval texts make clear that women did embroidery for their home and wore embroidered clothes. However, it is not clear how much was done and the practice may well have been less common than it was by the end of the sixteenth century.

The clothes of the period before 1500 do not exhibit much in the way of embroidery, or garments that could have been embroidered at home rather than in a professional workshop. From this period onwards, men's shirts and women's chemises start to be displayed at the neck and wrists, and these white linen surfaces offered ample opportunity for the domestic embroideress to embellish the cloth with all kinds of coloured, metallic and blackwork patterns, or with the new white cut-work 'lace'. The making of underwear appears to have been a female occupation, and mothers, wives and daughters seem to have made these garments at home until well into the nineteenth century. When embroidery began to appear on underwear it was probably quite natural for them to have sewn it. The degree to which these 'under-garments' were embroidered by the end of the sixteenth century would indicate both a large wealthy middle and upper class, and enough free time for the wives of professional, merchant and land-owning families to spend in this occupation. It perhaps fulfilled a need for more genteel pastimes for these women. This would mean something productive but not threatening to either the state or family, to replace the hard work they may have previously invested into their homes or their husbands' businesses, work now done by servants. For some individuals this took the form of an intense interest in religion, the only safe intellectual exercise that a woman could engage in (although there were limits to what was acceptable, as several women knew to their cost). Others found solace in embroidery.[23]

Opposite:
Sheep with letters on their rumps, 'B' or 'R S', which might be the initials of the embroiderer — detail from an embroidered picture, c. 1650-60.
(A. 1987. 143, see page 35)

However, it is rash to infer too much from the apparent lack of evidence for domestic embroidery before 1500, as there are few examples of household or personal clothing surviving before the sixteenth century. Church vestments and furnishings are, not surprisingly, rare because of the destruction meted out by the reformers and mobs during the Reformation in the mid-sixteenth century. Plain linen and large pieces of other fabric may well have been appropriated for use in people's houses as they could be recycled and made into new garments; and even linen altar cloths and towels could have found a new use in someone's home.

The overthrow of Roman Catholicism in England and Scotland must have left the professional embroidery workshops without the custom of ecclesiastics, or lay people requiring vestments as gifts for clergy or to enhance the churches. The use of vestments was forbidden by most of the Protestant denominations and many embroiderers would have been without a job. Even though church vestments formed a large part of the output of professional workshops, they also maintained their civilian ceremonial work, such as tabards for heralds, caps and palls for livery companies and robes for orders of chivalry.[24] The workshops also embroidered clothes for the nobility.

Contemporary literature and inventories suggest that clothing and household furnishings were often embroidered. In the detailed listings of work in the Royal Wardrobe accounts produced for the English kings and their families during the mediaeval period, embroidered items are mentioned many times. However, the accounts also indicate that fabric was often painted during this time and it is not always clear in illuminated manuscripts whether decorated fabrics were embroidered, painted or woven.

The rare survival of an undergarment such as St Louis's shirt in Notre-Dame Cathedral, Paris, indicates that very fine plain sewing was certainly achieved in this period. The gores at the sides of the shirt also have minute gathers at the top, done in a manner reminiscent of later smocking. The ability to embroider on clothes as well as 'to sew a fine seam' was apparent before the sixteenth century. All that is lacking today is the material evidence to show this.

Increased production of needlework in the home also required that suitable fabrics, threads and patterns were available to the embroideress, and that she had easy access to them. In the sixteenth century the spread of patterns was increased by the use of printed pattern books. A great number existed which gave needlewomen designs that could be used for all kinds of embroidery or for other forms of decoration within the home.[25] Other books were also illustrated, although it is doubtful if any man would have allowed his wife or daughter to deface a precious book to take patterns from the illustrations in them. From these books, which were translated and reprinted many times throughout the century and well into the next, women could select and record on pieces of linen any designs they wanted to use. They could try out new stitches or different colourways. Working them on fabric helped to bring the rather heavy black and white patterns to life, and must have enabled the embroideress to envisage new ways of using the designs. That so few of these books survive, despite being reprinted many times, suggests that they were well used to the point of destruction.

Rose – detail from a sampler by Martha Prescott, 1650. (A.1979.108, see page 32)

Pattern books would have appealed to professional embroiderers as well as to domestic workers. In the seventeenth century print sellers sold sheets of designs which could be used by various craftworkers. Several motifs common to embroideries of the period can be traced to these printed sheets, although again the sheets themselves are rare today.[26] The patterns were also drawn onto fabric for the embroideress to work on, and the print seller also sold them in this form.

The availability of materials is more difficult to determine, but the development of sheep with coarser and longer hair to produce worsted yarn is credited with the increased use of woollen threads in domestic embroidery.[27] Silk thread was always more expensive because, unlike wool, the raw material was not produced in Britain. A lot of silk was imported from Italy, although it was often dyed and made into sewing threads and fabric in Britain. The base fabric for domestic embroideries varied from canvas of hemp or linen, linen, fustian – a mixture of linen and cotton – and silk, depending on what the item was to be used for. Linen was grown in Britain, and canvas and fustian were probably also produced here. The finest linen, however, was manufactured in the Low Countries at this period, although this was more likely to be used for clothing.

Mercers in towns and cities sold fabrics and threads, but peddlers also travelled the countryside with goods for sale. Husbands, who were more likely to visit the towns, were often commissioned to buy needlework materials for their wives and daughters, with varying degrees of success. Even town-based family members

Sampler by Martha Prescott, 1650.
(A.1979.108)

might be called upon to buy supplies, and to furnish news on the latest fashions in both home decoration and clothing. Much thought and care went into the domestic needlework women produced for their homes, partly because of the expense, but also because they were the people who spent the greatest time in this environment and would have had to endure the results every day. That their husbands could be equally appreciative of their work is illustrated by Sir Walter Calverley's note in his diary for 1716. It records that his wife had finished the 'sewed' work in the drawing room and that it had taken her three and a half years to complete it.[28] Her panels can now be seen at Wallington in Northumberland where Lady Calverley's son took them when he moved.

Whilst some of the more elaborate work for both clothes and home furnishings after the mid-sixteenth century was probably still done by professionals, there was now more scope for the amateur to beautify her own home and family's clothes, to show her care for them, and to express some of her own artistic talents in the choice of motif, colours and stitches. Where and how she obtained her training in needlework is not always apparent, but from the late sixteenth century one of the ways she stored her knowledge survives in the form of the sampler.

SAMPLERS

Samplers are found in records before any dated examples appear. There is an entry in the Privy Purse expenses of Queen Elizabeth, wife of Henry VII of England, on 10 July 1502 for paying Thomas Fisshe eight pennies 'for an elne of lynnyn cloth for a sampler for the Quene'.[29] But the first sampler found in Britain, complete with a date, is the piece worked by Jane Bostocke in 1598 for her two-year old cousin Alice Lee.[30] Presumably this sampler was intended as a repertoire of stitches and patterns Alice could use when she was older. In between 1502 and 1598 there are references to samplers in works of literature and there are also existing samplers that could well be dated earlier than 1598.

Although the surviving samplers and the references to them in literature are for the amateur, the professional embroiderer must have used samplers as well. Embroiderers served apprenticeships like any other craft in the middle ages, and to acquire the necessary skills in stitching, design and layout they must have practised on small pieces of cloth. Early samplers are usually made up of different

motifs randomly scattered over the fabric. They often looked like the work of an apprentice or accomplished needlewoman practicing stitches and recording patterns. The ordered band samplers are much more likely to be the work of young girls learning a genteel craft.

One such sampler in the NMS collection (Accession number A.1979.108) is made of linen embroidered in coloured silks in double running, cross, eyelet hole, Montenegrin cross, needlelace and other stitches. It includes the worker's name, Martha Prescott, and the date 1650. The size is 200mm wide by 902mm long, the width of the linen cloth forming the length of the sampler. This is an elaborate band sampler of a very popular type in the seventeenth century. There are eleven different bands and an alphabet, done in eyelet holes. Samplers were not regularly named and dated at this period. The lower five panels are variations on a type that continued in Scottish samplers well into the nineteenth century – a flower with stems alternating as upright or reversed. The bands at the top of the sampler are more delicate border patterns, sewn in double running or Holbein stitch, and each separated by very narrow bands that were suitable for edging underwear or bed linen. The band third from the top has deer and a man holding a bird, whilst scattered around are other small animals including a frog, bird, mouse and insects. These are all common motifs on samplers of this date.[31] The prominent band in the centre of the sampler shows a white rose worked in needlelace stitches to make raised petals. The rose is crowned, with a rather soppy-faced lion on either side, and below each one is a woman in old-fashioned dress wearing a crown. To the left there is the letter 'E', and to the right 'R'. The whole band has a border at the top and bottom of alternating strawberries and acorns.

The same motif of the white rose flanked by crowned women was found on a sampler originally on loan to NMS, but later withdrawn and sold to a private collector. This sampler was dated 1659, but there was no name, only a set of initials – 'TF', 'IF', 'MF' and 'EF'. The story behind the piece is interesting. It had come into the lender's family through a marriage with an heiress named Weardon, probably in the early nineteenth century.[32]. It is also thought that the 'ER' (see above) represented Princess Elizabeth Stuart, better known as Elizabeth of Bohemia, the Winter Queen, and that the sampler was worked by her maids of honour. However, the 'ER' is more likely to stand for Queen Elizabeth, or possibly, because it is a white rose that has been worked, her grandmother, Elizabeth of York,

Rose, crowned women and 'ER' — detail from sampler by Martha Prescott, 1650.
(A.1979.108, see page 32)

wife of Henry VII of England. Prescott is also a Yorkshire surname. Regardless, because of the similarities between these two samplers it would appear that the same teacher taught the girls who worked them. In any case, their dates of 1650 and 1659 fall within the Commonwealth period when any indication of Royalty may not have been wise, so perhaps they were showing their Royalist allegiance by using the initials and symbol of a long dead queen.

The Victoria & Albert Museum owns samplers and a casket by Martha Edlin, and from the evidence of her samplers it is clear that girls might work more than one piece during their training. Martha Prescott's work, as discussed above, is a typical accomplished piece of embroidery, showing a variety of stitches and a degree of technical competence in needlework, even if the patterns are rather old-fashioned. The most obviously useful aspect of her sampler is the alphabet, because a woman would need to be able to mark her household and personal linen when she married and had her own home. Most embroidery by this period was done for wall hangings or bed curtains, together with matching cushions, caskets and boxes, or small decorative pictures for the wall. Very little embroidery appears

Embroidered picture,
c. *1650-60.*
(A.*1987.143*)

to have been worked on clothing, as braids, lace and ribbons were used in extravagant quantities from the 1640s onwards.

Quite when Martha Prescott would have used the border and band patterns she so laboriously worked is uncertain, but her small efforts at raised work would have meant that she could try something more ambitious such as the picture above (Accession number A.1987.143). On pale cream satin, it shows a wide range of stitches. The centre has an oval panel worked in very fine petit point, depicting a shepherd and shepherdess, a man fishing in a pond, and a group of buildings in the background. The oval is outlined in a scrolled border. On either side are two figures in raised work. There is a women on the left with a satin embroidered dress

imitating floral silk, and a deep collar and cuffs in needlelace. Her face and hands are of padded pink satin and her hair has been worked in looped stitches. She holds a vine branch with a bunch of grapes worked in different techniques. Opposite her is a young man wearing a pale beige doublet and wide-legged breeches with a profusion of ribbon bows, a black hat, gloves and pink jacket, all worked in needlelace stitches. The rest of the panel is crowded with bunches of flowers worked in rococo stitch, a pear tree and a hazel tree with three-dimensional fruit, a building with mica windows standing on a green lawn, butterflies, caterpillars, a leopard, deer and a parrot on a tree stump. There is also a pool surrounded by rocks in purl stitch, a rabbit chased by a hound, and a tulip and rose with three-dimensional petals. This piece was acquired by private treaty sale and originally came from the collection of Sir Frederick Richmond.

Certain motifs were obviously popular. The figures of men and women, for example, gave great scope for loving details of their clothes to be worked. The fruit of trees and peas in their pods were other recurring themes. The large flowers that appear so out of scale to the other motifs are usually taken from printed sheets, whilst the animals found in the corners of the embroidered panels usually include a lion, leopard, deer and rabbit – although not exclusively. These three-dimensional and needlelace techniques were often used on the embroidered caskets which are so much a feature of the mid to late-seventeenth century. NMS owns about five in various conditions. The best preserved example, however, does not have any of these elaborate techniques.

Fashionably dressed man – detail from embroidered picture, c. 1650-60. (A.1987.143, see page 35)

CASKETS

NMS's best preserved casket (Accession number A.1961.502) has a wooden carcass covered in white linen and stiff white paper, embroidered in coloured silks, silver and silver-gilt threads in satin stitch and couched-work. Its height is 320mm, width 260mm, depth 178mm, and it dates to about 1650-80. It was bought from John Bell of Aberdeen.

The casket is a double one with hipped top standing on four brown wood ball feet. There are two front doors, embroidered with a man on the left door and a woman on the right, both with buildings in the background. On the top is a man playing a pipe and a woman fishing in a pool, with two buildings behind them and the sun

Opposite: Embroidered casket, c. 1660-80. (A.1961.502)

peeping out from the clouds. These motifs were very common during this period and are frequently found on caskets and pictures.[33] The figures are related to those depicted in one of the pattern books, *The Needles Excellency*, published in 1631. On the slope of the front of the casket are a lion, leopard, rabbit and dog. The back and sides are covered with silk threads in geometric laid work patterns worked on thick paper, and these were probably sewn by a professional, perhaps working for the cabinet maker.

The casket is lined in a very thin pink silk typical of other caskets. Also typical are the silver metal braid edging to the panels, stamped borders to the drawer edges, four bun feet, silver metal carrying handles at the sides, and the hinges and lock plates. There are two main components that open to reveal the compartments and drawers. The top has a hinged lid containing a mirror that can be taken out. The top compartment has a removable pen tray with inkwell and pounce pot for sand at either end, and a shallow hollow below. At the back is a narrow space where a needle case probably sat. Along the left are two glass bottles with pewter screw stoppers, probably for scented water, whilst on the right is a rectangular red velvet pin cushion which lifts out to reveal a secret drawer in its lower part. In the centre is a rectangular well covered in silk.

Behind the doors at the front of the casket is a long drawer across the full width of the bottom, and above it three smaller drawers. The two on the right are shorter, and the division between them pulls out to reveal another secret drawer with narrow divisions, probably intended for rings. The whole top of the casket is hinged and when opened it reveals another shallow compartment. By pressing on a catch behind the lock, the front panel above the lower drawers slides up to reveal three more small drawers. When the two right-hand ones are removed, a further secret drawer is revealed.

Caskets were a particular feature of mid-seventeenth century needlework and appear to have been fashionable items. Many survive, but few in such good condition as this example. They rarely contain any information on their maker or subsequent owners, and dates or names appear on only a few pieces. Although this casket was bought from a dealer in Aberdeen, there is no certainty that it originally came from a Scottish source. However, in an inventory for Hamilton Palace, made in 1681, the contents of Lady Katherine's room include 'an embroidered cabinet' which is possibly a reference to just such a casket. Lady Katherine was the eldest daughter of the third Duke and Duchess of Hamilton, born in 1662. She married Lord Murray, later first Duke of Atholl, in 1683.[34]

The embroiderers of these caskets appear to have been young girls. The embroidery was first done on the linen or satin ground and then applied to a wooden carcass, which was made to fit the work by a joiner or cabinet maker. The carcasses are fairly crude affairs. Many of the boxes had their own travelling cases, sometimes almost as crude as the box itself, but there are instances where a more ornate case of polished and inlaid wood or stamped leather has survived. To protect the embroidery in the travelling case a fine silk cover was made. Although these caskets survive in quite large numbers, very few have retained their cases, probably because they were so crudely made. Even fewer examples retain their silk covers.

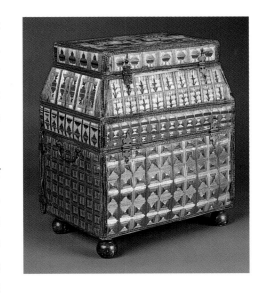

The side and back of the casket showing the geometric patterns. (A.1961.502)

The casket open to show the secret drawers.

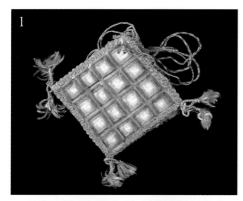

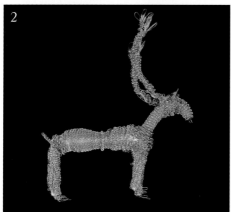

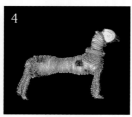

The NMS casket is in such wonderful condition that it must originally have had a travelling case and silk cover, otherwise it is unlikely to have survived with its embroidery still so bright. There are also indications that the geometric embroidery was originally covered by mica. There are no initials or dates on the casket to inform us who made it or where she lived. There is, however, a possible clue to its date on the reverse of the sliding panel. On the blue paper backing, someone has written later in pencil a few dates that appear to be sums reckoning the number of years since 1678. This may indicate that at some time there was a dated letter, or that the original maker was known.

This casket is very similar in construction, fittings and style of embroidery to the example by Hannah Smith in the Whitworth Art Gallery, Manchester.[35] Hannah's casket is also one of the very few of which the maker and date are known. She finished her work on the piece whilst staying in Oxford around 1654, between the ages of 12 and 14, and she had the casket made up in London when she went there two years later. Disappointingly, there appears to be no more information about Hannah or her family, so it is not known if she came from a professional, merchant or land-owning background. Nor is anything documented at present about Martha Edlin who, in 1671, when eleven, made a similar casket. This example is now in the Victoria & Albert Museum.[36] Stored inside were two samplers – a coloured band sampler done in 1668 and one of white work dated 1673. She also made a beadwork jewel case in the same year. By the age of 13 it was obvious that Martha was a formidably accomplished needlewoman.

Inside the NMS casket several sewing accessories were found. There were also some 'toys', probably contemporary with the piece; as well as two small oval ivory plaques painted in sepia with a woman and birds, which date to the late eighteenth or early nineteenth century. One of the 'toys' is a nut, perhaps a nutmeg, hollowed

'Toys' from casket:

1 *Square purse. (A.1961.502A)*
2 *Stag. (A.1961.502B)*
3 *Snake. (A.1961.502C)*
4 *Hound. (A.1961.502D)*
5 *Carnation. (A.1961.502F)*
6 *Strawberry flowers worked in needlelace. (A.1961.502E)*
7 *Nut with inscriptions on paper streamers. (A.1961.502G)*
8 *Combined pincushion and purse. (A.1961.502I)*
9 *Purse. (A.1961.502J)*
10 *Pincushion with bead lattice cover. (A.1961.502K)*

out and covered in a network of silver and coloured silks. Wound up inside are two long paper tapes with the following inscriptions written in ink:

1 *The God above vouchsafeth store. To him in fault that prayeth therefore: But for his quifts you thankless run: Their wealth shall waste as wax in Sunn.*

2 *Ask what thou wilt and though shalt have; if though in Christ yu same do crave: For Christ thy mediator sees when tough to him doest fall in knees.*

There were also two pincushions of red velvet with plaited red silk cords and a metal loop handle. One of them is circular with a purse attached. The other is rectangular red linen, tightly stuffed, with one side covered in gilt metal foil over which a network of blue, amber, yellow and white beads is attached. There is a flap with hanging ring at one end.[37]

A square purse was also found. It consists of two flat cards covered in coloured silk laid-work like the casket, with a small silk bag in between, set with the opening on a point of the square. This type may have been used for scented herbs rather than money, which no young woman at this period would have carried.[38]

The 'toys' include three animals made out of silver metal coiled thread wound round a solid core covered in silk threads. The animals may have been intended to be added to another embroidery or basket as three-dimensional pieces. The stag and dog would have been part of a chase scene, and the snake could well have been intended for inclusion in a representation of Adam and Eve (Genesis 3).[39] Two other items that could well have been destined for another embroidery are a carnation and a bunch of flowers. These are worked in coloured silk threads.

There are two types of caskets: a double one described above, and a large flat rectangular box. The double caskets were used for storing writing materials and some personal grooming aids, with spaces for jewellery and other small treasures. They were fitted with keys, one for the lid and one for the doors at the front of the casket. The layout of these caskets is so similar that there must have been a standard pattern. The secret drawers would not have fooled anyone who had seen one before, but the casket was still a coveted hiding place for a teenage girl's treasures. It would remain with her when she married, as she continued to hoard all those small trinkets that mattered.

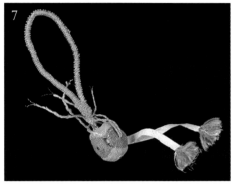

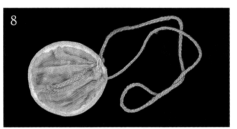

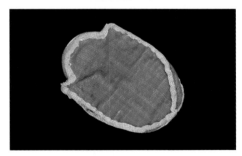

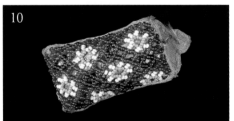

EMBROIDERED TEXTILES

BY the time a girl had finished her embroidery training she would be capable of doing all the embroidered furnishings for the home. Some of the pieces referred to in this chapter may not have been worked in a domestic situation, but they are all examples of embroidery that were typical of the work of amateur needlewomen. In the next chapter the work of professional embroiderers will be featured.

EMBROIDERED HANGINGS

By the seventeenth century embroidered wall and bed hangings were fairly common and various styles evolved, their use depending on the purse of the owner. One type involved embroidering small motifs on canvas which could then be applied to velvet or wool. This saved on the cost of embroidering whole curtains, but it also meant that the small 'slips', as they were known, could be worked comfortably in the hand without a frame if necessary. The Oxburgh hangings worked by Mary, Queen of Scots and Bess of Hardwick are examples of this type, where the small motifs, individually worked on canvas, were then sewn on to a velvet background.[40]

A panel of embroidery, unused, was acquired by NMS in 1975.[41] It is probably an example of 'pillar work', a term found in inventories to describe a type of embroidery on hangings. The NMS panel (Accession number K.2000.645) consists of four upright trees set on a mound, with an animal at each base typical of those on sixteenth and seventeenth-century embroideries – a lion and three rabbits. Each tree bears stylised pomegranates, carnations, grapes, columbine and other typical flowers and fruit, all drawn in a very naïve style and worked in cross-stitch over two threads, in wool and some silk. The individual trees are worked on a separate strip of canvas, which is probably of hemp, about 1705mm by 265mm, and they were almost certainly intended to be sewn as separate elements down curtain edges. This panel was recorded as belonging to Lady Gordon of Park, Banffshire, the last individual bearing this name being Joanna, who died in 1872. NMS bought them from the sale of the W S Bell collection, Aberdeen, in 1975.

Opposite:
Figures in Turkish style dress within a rocky base – detail from a crewel-work hanging, late 17th or early 18th century.
(K.2000.556, see page 49)

Crewelwork hanging worked in red wool, early 17th century. (A.1930.708)

Detail from the same piece.

Crewelwork

Crewelwork is the name applied to embroidery done in wool. The term is derived from the thin worsted yarn used to embroider on a linen or fustian ground. Fustian is a mixed cotton and linen fabric. The exact origin of the word 'crewelwork' is unknown. The most usual surviving forms are the large hangings and curtains, often worked with large fleshy leaves or the 'Tree of Life' motif, dating from the seventeenth and early eighteenth centuries. However, the term may also be applied to other types of embroidery.

Wool was a cheaper thread to use on large household textiles than silk. It also took colour well and was easier to dye than linen. This gave the embroideress scope for making very colourful designs. Wool could also be obtained in threads of varying degrees of fineness to suit the purse of the maker, and a coarser thread meant that the work could be completed more quickly. All these points probably help to explain its use in the seventeenth century when the fashion for embroidered hangings became popular. There was also a long tradition of wool embroidery in northern Europe, where it was the dominant fibre. One of the most famous embroideries of the mediaeval period, the Bayeaux 'Tapestry', is a crewelwork piece, although it was probably produced in a professional workshop in Kent. It is now the only surviving piece that can give some idea of what was obviously a well-known form of furnishing textile from the late Saxon to early Norman period in England.

NMS has several examples of crewelwork hangings, the most spectacular being two wall hangings and four valances dated 1719, acquired in 1988 and described on pages 53-7. These formed the centrepiece of the NMS exhibition and were shown with other examples that illustrated the diversity of design used in this medium over the seventeenth and early eighteenth centuries.

Two early to mid-seventeenth century examples described here illustrate that crewelwork did not have to be heavy in its design. Both are airy patterns with much open space left on the white fustian ground. The warps, the vertical threads on a loom, that required to be the stronger, were usually in linen, with the wefts, the horizontal threads, being of cotton. Both these earlier crewelwork hangings are worked in one colour with a variety of stitches.

One of these panels (Accession number A.1930.708) is embroidered with a design of exotic-looking flowers, each within a coiling tendril of a stem that joins the

Crewelwork hanging,
worked in blue wool,
early to mid 17th century,
and a detail from the
same piece.
(A.1926.153)

different motifs together. These are very reminiscent of the flowers within curling stems found on late sixteenth and early seventeenth-century embroideries for women's caps and bodices. At the bottom is a border design of smaller flower heads, divided from their neighbour by a scalloped arcade. Another piece of this pattern was bought by the Victoria & Albert Museum.[42] A very similar design of flowers with a border pattern can be seen on a piece now made into a petticoat in the Museum of London.[43] The NMS panel is made of three widths of fustian only 430mm wide, the height being 2010mm. The embroidery has been worked in red wool in stem stitch with speckling and French knots. The design had been drawn on the fabric in outline only, finishing before the top, and some of the flowers have not been worked exactly as drawn. The edges are finished with a red and white braid and the embroidery is lined with cotton, possibly of a later date. The panel was bought from a dealer and nothing is known of its history. However, written in a nineteenth-century hand on the back in ink is the word 'Flyfield', which could be a person or place.

The other panel (Accession number A.1926.153) also has a companion piece in the Victoria & Albert Museum.[44] The design is worked in blue, a repeating pattern of ogees containing a vase of flowers. In the centre of the vase there is a rose with tulips, pansy, honeysuckle and carnation and other flowers, all standard motifs found on sixteenth and early seventeenth-century domestic and personal embroidered items. The fabric width is 505mm and there are four used for the panel. Its height is 1780mm and it is backed in plain linen with twelve original tape loops across the top and twelve replacements, to hang the piece on the wall or from a rod around a bed. Matching valances would originally have hidden the loops. Both these early pieces are likely to have been bed curtains, because of the lightness of their design, but when the original method of hanging a panel is no longer evident it can be difficult to determine where in a room a piece went. Bed curtains appear to have been made of two wide curtains for the sides and two narrower curtains for the foot end of the bed, the head end having a cloth or wooden panel.

A later seventeenth-century panel has a wonderful all-over design of large exotic leaves on a heavy central stem, worked in shades of blue that have not faded (Accession number A.1925.415). The design is contained within the size of the panel — two widths of 510mm and one of 260mm of weft-faced twill 1980mm high. Traces of the original drawing are visible at the sides. The stitches used include stem, long and short, fly, coral, basket, buttonhole and seed. The panel is edged with blue braid, and a knotted linen fringe is sewn along the sides and lower edge. At the top are eight out of twelve linen tape loops for hanging. This piece was bought from the Royal School of Needlework and it has undergone restoration in the past. However, it would appear to be basically as it was originally made and is

Opposite:
Crewelwork hanging with large fleshy leaves, worked in shades of blue wool, mid to late 17th century.
(A.1925.415)

Details from the same piece showing the stitching.

likely to have been a bed or window curtain. Window curtains were not so common in the seventeenth century as they became later, but they do occur in inventories and were often made to match the bed curtains.

Later in the nineteenth and early twentieth centuries there was a fashion for reusing crewelwork as bed curtains for the four-poster beds in vogue at that time. Often the ground fabric had deteriorated or discoloured, so the embroidery was re-applied to a new ground and made to fit the required size of curtain. The most common pattern to be treated in this way is the variety known as the 'Tree of Life'. This shows a large tree growing from a small mound at the bottom of the panel, its branches curving up and across the width, with exotic leaves and flowers and perhaps a very detailed landscape at the base. This was an extremely popular motif and panels from many sets exist. They can be seen in country houses and museum collections all over the country.

NMS bought a panel of crewelwork at the sale at Cullen House, Banffshire, in 1975 and this is one such piece that has been re-applied to a new ground (Accession number K.2000.556).[45] In this case it had become a bedspread with new borders of green velvet and a ground of shiny furnishing satin.[46] The panel, dating to the late seventeenth or early eighteenth century, is worked in fairly coarse wool in long and short stitches and French knots. The embroidery has been re-applied to a cream twill cotton sateen ground in the early twentieth century. The present size is now 1765mm width by 2280mm in length. The design consists of three trees that grow out of a rocky landscape where various hollows are filled with figures in vaguely Turkish or Indian dress, including a shepherd piping to his flock, deer, rabbits, dogs and a leopard. Above, the branches are covered in large fleshy curving leaves and exotic flowers. Some of them are reminiscent of the earlier seventeenth-century flowers found on embroideries, such as the rose, carnation and lily. The embroidery is densely worked and the rocks are done in French knots.

This panel is closely related to three painted and dyed cotton hangings made in western India for the European market. Originally from Ashburnham House, Sussex, they were sold in 1952, together with a set of four chain-stitched curtains also made in India, and a palampore, all with the same pattern. These pieces are now split between the Victoria & Albert Museum, London, the Museum of Fine Arts, Boston, the Cooper Hewitt Museum, New York, and the Calico Museum,

Opposite:
Crewelwork hanging from Cullen House, Banffshire, with a 'Tree of Life' motif, late 17th or early 18th century.
(K.2000.556)

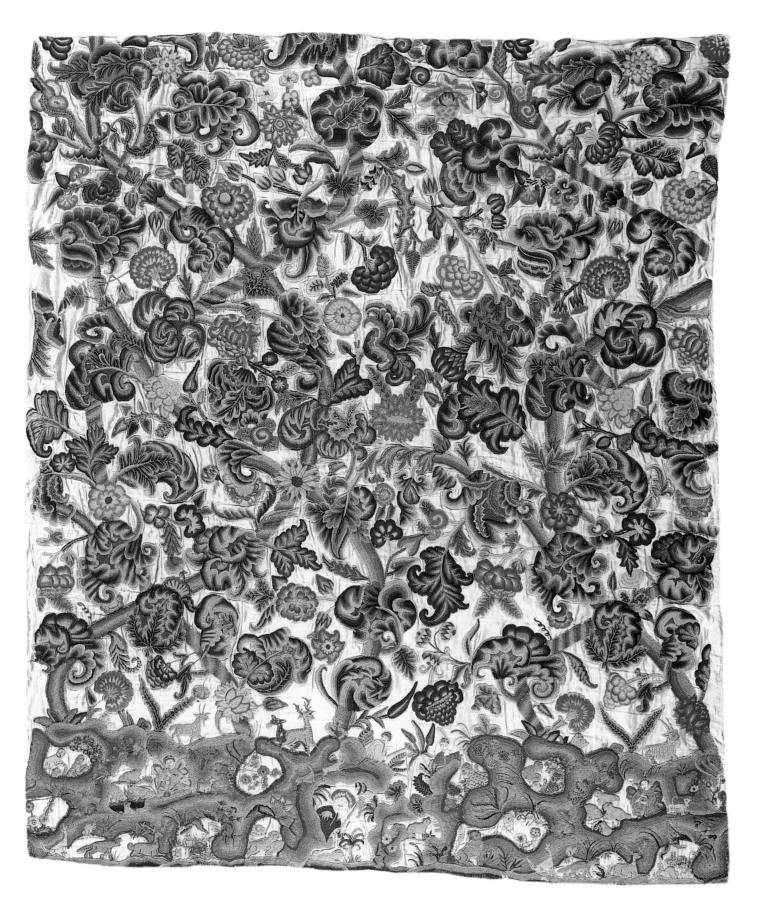

Ahmedabad.[47] In addition there is a very similar panel in crewelwork, but not from the same set as NMS, in the Burrell Collection, Glasgow [48], and a fragment of a third panel in Boston (Accession number 53.172) of crewelwork that matches neither the Burrell nor the NMS pieces. In addition there is a panel with a very similar rocky base but no figures in the Philadelphia Museum of Art (Accession number 1996-107-3). Irwin and Brett, in their book on *The Origins of Chintz*, consider that the source, from which the pattern was derived, was probably a printed one published in England for embroideries. The survival of three crewelwork panels, all from different sets of the same design, suggests that this is the case. So far it appears to be the most numerous single design of the very popular 'Tree of Life' motif, and shows how an embroideress could add individuality to the same outline by her choice of additional elements, colours and stitches.

A more usual treatment of the 'Tree of Life' motif is that found on another panel in the NMS collection (Accession number A.1955.120). This is worked on a twill weave fustian ground, in bright wools in long and short, using stem and basket stitches, with the trees growing out of green hillocks and two deer running along the bottom. The leaves are the usual large fleshy, curling ones, with various flowers, exotic birds and squirrels in the branches. One of the problems with this kind of embroidery shows clearly on this piece, and that is the tendency for the fabric to pucker, because the wool is too coarse to go smoothly through the tightly

Painted and dyed cotton hanging made for the European market, based on the same source as the hanging from Cullen House, see page 50. Western India, late 17th or early 18th century. (© Victoria and Albert Museum IS156-1953)

Opposite:
Crewelwork hanging with the 'Tree of Life' pattern, late 17th century. (A.1955.120)

52

woven cloth. In comparison to the 1719 hangings this is a competent piece, but not a *tour de force*. Nonetheless, this simple but colourful basic design would have brightened up any dark castle or house wall.

The most magnificent example of the 'Tree of Life' pattern in the NMS collection are the two wall hangings and four valances acquired at auction in 1988 with the generous support of the National Art Collections Fund (Accession number A.1988.263 A-E). Made of white twill weave linen, they are embroidered in coloured wools and silks in long and short and chain stitches and French knots. On one of the valances is the monogram 'IRCR' of the Old Pretender, James Francis Edward Stewart, and his wife Clementina Sobeiska. It also includes the date of their marriage, '1719'.

The hangings are made up of four widths of narrow twill weave white linen of fine quality, joined together by over-sewing. They are embroidered with the 'Tree of Life' design, which has been drawn in ink on the linen in outline only; the maker has done the shading and other embellishments. The threads used are of good quality crewel wool and there is no variation in the colours, suggesting either very good dyers with quality control, or else that all the threads needed were bought at the same time.

The two large panels have a deep border, worked in a very dense manner with various vignettes, including a deer being chased by a hound, a large sunflower, a

Opposite:
One of two crewelwork wall hangings with the 'Tree of Life' pattern, dated 1719.
(A.1988.263A)

Monogram 'IRCR' and '1719 on one of the valances.
(A.1988.263 C)

frog by a pond, a squirrel, a rabbit, and a devil playing the bagpipes. The valances all have flowers. One contains a sunflower, its centre embroidered with the crowned monogram 'IRCR, 1719' mentioned above. This device is not placed centrally and may have been intended to be inconspicuous in the final plan of the room for which these hangings were made. One of the valances has been added to the top of one of the hangings, probably at a later date. Originally, valances would have hidden the hooks that were used to hang the embroideries on the wall. That these examples were intended to be hung is confirmed by three rows of small brass rings knotted into a tape running down the back of each panel. These were attached to hooks fitted on to the wall to stop the hangings flapping.

These embroideries are particularly striking examples of crewelwork. The freshness of the colours and the exuberance of the design are especially notable. The tree trunks are all shaded, something the maker has devised for herself. On the top she has sewn small wisps of green for ferns or moss. Indeed there is an almost obsessive wish to cover the ground as closely as possible. The centres of the flowers are worked in French knots so tightly packed that every warp and weft has been pierced, and some flower centres are in danger of falling out because there is no ground left to support them. The density of stitches on the border is also more than required and again the whole border could fall away. Within the main design there are birds and flowers stuck on to the branches of the trees at odd angles, as if the embroideress had found a space and felt compelled to fill it. Perhaps she was driven by a compulsion to embroider or to keep herself occupied.

It is clear that the above examples are the work of an amateur embroiderer and not a professional workshop, because no one could have afforded to pay a workshop for such an elaborate piece. There appears to have been only one hand working on the hangings and it is an idiosyncratic style. The linen may have been bought marked out, but the embroideress must have acquired it from a merchant who imported good quality linen from Holland. The local weavers in Scotland probably could not produce such quality at that time. Although the basic design might have been acquired from an outside source, the embellishments were most likely added in by the embroiderer. The deer and hound are very typical motifs found on samplers and other embroideries. The flowers, such as the Crown Imperial, could have been drawn from a printed sheet or other illustration, but the rather ornithologically suspect birds may well have been copied from another embroidery or piece of

*Hound chasing a deer —
detail from the crewelwork
wall hanging, dated 1719.
(A.1988.263 A, see page 52)*

fabric. Although some of the flowers and animals are very recognisable, others show that the maker has possibly never observed an example of what she has worked. The squirrel, for example, has a green tail, a feature that is unlikely to have been incorporated if a more accurate likeness had been witnessed.

The set of hangings is probably incomplete. Although there are four valances, there may not have been four panels of similar size, as there would have been windows and a fireplace to consider. The hangings were not lined before the rings were knotted in, but the edges have been bound with tape, except for the top one which was not finished. There is no indication as to how they would have been hung. The valances have not been finished with tape, although they have been turned up in readiness. Originally these hangings must have been made for a specific room in a particular house and would have hung about 700-800mm from the floor, so that the amazing border design could be seen.

There is no evidence as to who made these pieces, except it must have been a Jacobite supporter. The monogram on the hanging is also found on medals struck

to commemorate the marriage of James Stewart and Clementina in Rome in 1719. However, the hangings were not made for this occasion. The embroideress probably incorporated the date and monograph when she heard of the marriage. The sunflower was used as the symbol of a special relationship between a faithful subject and a sovereign who was also his patron. It was used in this way by Sir Anthony Van Dyke in his self-portrait, probably painted after he was knighted in 1632; and also in his portrait of Sir Kenelm Digby of the same period.[49]

The internal evidence of the quality of the cloth and threads, as well as the size of the whole scheme, suggests that a wife rather than a daughter made this piece. She might have been married to a wealthy man who had business in London, where power was based by this time. He probably left his wife on their Scottish estates for long periods while he attended to matters of business down south. These estates may not have been near a major centre of social activity, and there were probably enough servants so that she did not have to be an active housekeeper. This may have driven her to create these beautiful hangings, which are far more lavishly worked than strictly necessary. She may have been a workaholic, but she certainly knew how to compose a pleasing and harmonious scheme for her room hangings.

Around 1719, who among the Jacobite families might have made these? The only possible clue is to be found on the collars of the embroidered hounds where 'AV' appears to have been worked in Gothic script, a feature of contemporary samplers.

Although it might be expected that a Scottish embroideress would incorporate her own initials (women did not relinquish their own name after marriage in Scotland), as they are on a dog's collar it would be more logical for them to be those of her husband. 'V' was used at this period for a 'U' and the most obvious Scottish surname starting with 'U' is 'Urquhart'. One possibility is Alexander Urquhart of Newhall. In 1716 he married Anne Hamilton, daughter of Colonel Thomas Hamilton of Olivestob, Haddington. He was Member of Parliament for Cromartyshire from 1715 to 1722, and for Ross from 1722 to 1727, being returned as a Whig on the recommendation of the Duke of Montrose, Secretary for Scotland. However, he voted against the government on all recorded divisions and professed 'great zeal' for the Old Pretender's service, becoming well known to the Duke of Sunderland, for whom he acted as an intermediary with the Jacobites. He received a commission as a lieutenant colonel from James in 1722. However, after Sunderland's death Urquhart became dependent on the Whig minister, Robert Walpole, and his speculation in the ill-fated South Sea Bubble scheme (1719-21) led to his eventual downfall.[50]

Urquhart appears to have had a very complicated series of financial transactions and invested for others, lending and borrowing money with which to buy stock. Walpole seems to have abandoned Urquhart and forced him to renounce his parliamentary immunity so that his creditors could press for their money. He died intestate in 1727, and Newhall, which he had built, and where these hangings were possibly destined to go, passed to his principal creditors and relations, the Gordons of Invergordon. There is a drawing of the new house built by Alexander Urquhart and this shows a typical late seventeenth to early eighteenth-century house of two storeys and a basement with steeply pitched roof and dormer windows.[51] The present house was built c.1805. Urquhart and his wife had a son and daughter who both married, and one unmarried daughter, but it would appear there were no descendants who could have inherited these hangings.[52] In the early 1900s a family in Aberdeen owned them, but there is no information as to how they were acquired.

Alexander Urquhart conforms to all the criteria that would facilitate the making of these hangings. Whilst it is doubtful whether it can ever be proved that Anne Hamilton, wife of Alexander Urquhart, made these pieces, her name is put forward as at least a possibility for the identity of the embroideress who created one of the most stunning pieces of domestic needlework to survive in Britain.

Tulips – detail from the second of the two 1719 hangings.
(A.1988.263 B)

The 'Tree of Life' as a motif enjoyed a revival in the late nineteenth century with the fashion for mediaeval-style furnishings. NMS owns a bedspread, side curtains, back hanging and pelmet, designed by the Scottish architect Sir Robert Lorimer, and donated by his son Christopher Lorimer in 1984 (Accession number H.SLV31 A-D). The bedspread, 2630mm by 2090mm, is worked in pastel shades of wool on linen, and has as the central motif a tree with exotic leaves and flowers, growing from a mound of earth. Deer skip along the bottom, while birds with vicious hooked beaks sit on the branches. Below this appears a long poem. The piece is dated 1897 above a shield with a cross. The complete set is believed to have been worked by Jeannie Skinner, the local postmistress at Arncroach, and was intended for Gibliston House, Fife.

The example of crewelwork in the NMS collection that shows elements of old and new motifs is probably a bed cover as it is nearly square, 1525mm by 1475mm. The design has a central motif with a border all round (Accession number A.1949.224). Worked on white fustian with a twill weave, it has at its centre a fashionably-dressed man and woman as shepherd and shepherdess, with a dog and sheep, surrounded by wavy stems with exotic flowers and leaves, repeated in the border. In the corners are four animals – a stag, leopard, lion and peacock – exactly as found on many of the mid seventeenth-century embroideries. Dating to *c.*1700, there is a certain naïvety about this piece, but it is well worked in brightly-coloured wools.

59

Crewelwork hanging
with a 'Tree of Life' design
influenced by Indian
styles, early 18th century.
(A.1964.508)

60

Another interpretation of the 'Tree of Life' design owes something to the contemporary taste for Indian textiles (Accession number A.1964.508). The ground is white linen with a lighter, slender tree, the branches curving down to the ground and up to the top of the panel, with deeply serrated leaves and various exotic flowers. In the branches are birds with long tails. The embroidery is in bright wools, predominantly red and green, mainly in stem and long and short stitches. A border has been sewn with similar flowers and leaves on a smaller scale, and at the top a plain linen band has been added. The panel is made up of two and a half widths of 860mm wide linen and is 2145mm in height, but it has been trimmed at the right and is missing about 530mm at the side. It is lined and has brass rings at the top.

Three panels, three bases and three top valances from this set are now in the Fitzwilliam Museum, Cambridge.[53] All these pieces were originally on loan to the Royal Scottish Museum from 1934-47, when one panel and one valance were left with the museum and the rest went on loan to Cambridge. Both museums subsequently acquired them. They were lent by Lady Ingram, wife of Sir Bruce Ingram, as the correspondence in the museum files makes clear, but there is no indication of whether they were family pieces or not. The embroideries as they now exist were probably a set of bed curtains, but it is obvious that they had been converted to fit a taller bed in later life by the addition of the pieces to top and bottom. In 1938 the complete set was lent to the Empire Exhibition in Glasgow and used in a period room, the last time all the embroideries were shown in this way.

A completely new design for crewelwork is represented by a panel in NMS (Accession number A.1928.169), of which another, larger, panel is in the Victoria & Albert Museum, together with some lengths of border. Two additional panels are in the National Museum of Wales in Cardiff.[54] The design consists of a border on three sides of ogival compartments alternating with a bunch of carnations and harebells tied with a ribbon and sprays of berberis. In between there are strapwork panels in red, and curling green leaves with a rope border on either side of the whole design. Down the centre are individual sprays of mixed flowers, including roses, harebells, carnations and lilies. There is a red cotton border and backing that appear to be modern.

The panel in the Victoria & Albert Museum contains the words: 'Yt was begun April the 22 1729.' It is thought to have been made by Rachel, daughter of Vincent

Detail of the piece opposite.

Crewelwork hanging, dated 1729. (A.1928.169)

61

Detail of the crewelwork hanging on page 61.

Detail of the piece opposite.

Corbet of Ynysmaengwyn, near Towyn, Merionth. Little is known of Rachel apart from the fact that she was the youngest of four children of Vincent and Ann Corbet. Her sister Ann inherited the estate in 1723 and started to build a new house in 1730, which still stands. The family, however, sold the estate in 1874.[55] NMS bought its panel from the Royal School of Needlework, as did the Victoria & Albert Museum, but the border lengths were donated many years later by Joan Evans. The National Museum of Wales acquired its panels in 1954, and these do not appear to have been with the other panels in 1928. It is not clear if they are bed or window curtains, or wall hangings.

QUILTS

Quilting, where two layers of fabric enclose a soft filling and then all three layers are held together by stitching, has a very long history and has been used by many different cultures for both protection and warmth. In Britain various types of quilting were used for bed covers. Quilting is often combined with patchwork, another form of needlework used to create bed covers. Although perhaps considered as a form of thrift, patchwork could in fact be expensive as specially printed cotton pieces were often bought to act as a centrepiece to a quilt. To create a truly decorative and aethestically pleasing effect on a piece of patchwork, it was often necessary to have enough fabric to complete the pattern undertaken. This might require buying fabric, rather than using leftovers from dressmaking or cutting up old clothes.

NMS has a few patchwork covers and only one or two quilts, but there are three embroidered covers that have been quilted. The earliest example is made of fine linen embroidered all over with small floral motifs and a few birds (Accession number A.1985.217). It has been designed in a British copy of the Mogul style in red and green silk, worked in chain stitch, possibly tamboured, and including the signature 'ER 1690'. The top and sides of the cover are in plain linen, and the whole is then quilted in an elaborate design of a circle, with tulip and daisy heads in the centre and interlace around it. Both the top and the back of the quilt are pieced, and the wadding is also different in the centre to that at the sides. The style of the quilting patterns suggests that it was done in the later eighteenth century. It therefore appears that the quilt has been made up from the best pieces of an original 1690 embroidered quilt, with plain linen added to make up the size.

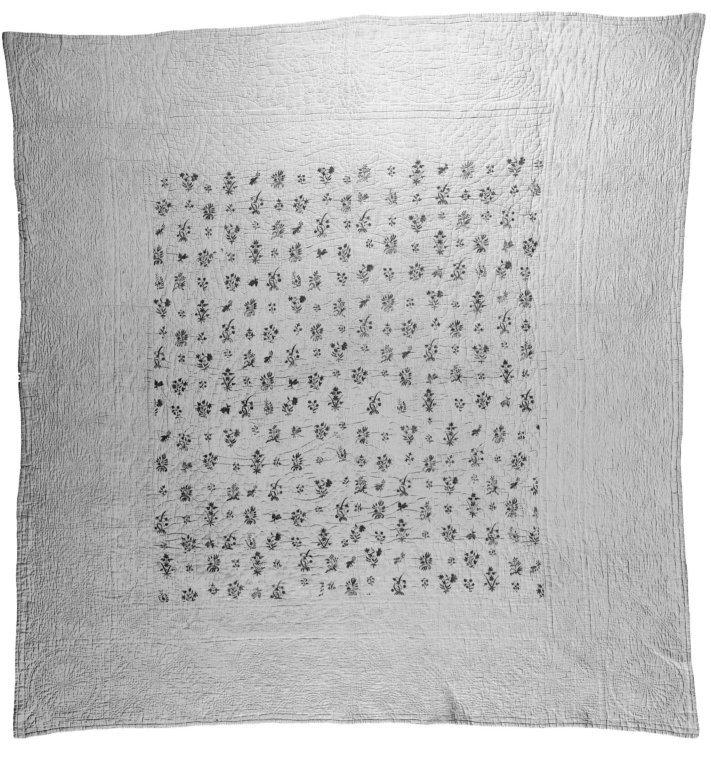

*Embroidered and quilted
bed cover, the embroidery
dated 1690, the quilt
design late 18th century.
(A.1985.217)*

Corner of embroidered and quilted bed cover showing the initials 'AC' and date, '1749'. (K.1998.1166)

Embroidered and quilted bed cover, with printed linen borders, 1795. (A.1929.573)

Embroidery pattern and printed border – detail of the same piece.

The whole was then re-quilted with a new design, using fairly coarse white linen thread to sew it.[56]

A plainer embroidered quilt in NMS's collection is dated '1749' and has the initials 'AC', both worked in eyelet hole stitch (Accession number K.1998.1166). The top is of white linen embroidered with coloured wools, with a border pattern of flower plants in diamonds, and small birds and animals in the triangles in between. In each corner is a heart shape with a flowering plant and there are also four of these in the centre. This is a naïve design but fascinating given its date, for many of the motifs found on samplers throughout the seventeenth century are ultimately derived from sixteenth-century pattern books. These patterns survived in samplers made in Scotland until well into the nineteenth century, and the use of eyelet holes to work the initials and date suggests this quilt was indeed Scottish. It is a well-used piece and may have been made for her trousseau by 'AC'.

From the period at the end of the eighteenth century, NMS has a quilt with the initials 'MB 1795' worked in blue (Accession number A.1929.573). Made of white linen, it is embroidered in coloured wools in chain stitch with a border of trailing flowers and scallops. The centre is scattered with floral sprays. The sides have been extended with printed linen in a small purple trailing pattern. The way the embroidery is laid out suggests this quilt has also been made up from an earlier piece, which

has then been put together and quilted. The printed linen was possibly added later still. The quilting design is similar to that on the example discussed earlier.

Patchwork has experienced a renaissance in the last twenty years, but the pieces produced are not always household items. One recent acquisition by NMS is a panel worked by the contemporary patchwork artist, Pauline Burbidge (Accession number K.1999.945). This piece is an example of combining both patchwork and quilting in a modern interpretation of these old techniques to create a striking wall hanging. In the

Patchwork wall hanging
'Dancing Lines' by
Pauline Burbidge, 1998.
(K.1999.945)

66

Scottish Development Agency's crafts collection there is a more traditional bed quilt by Moira Robertson. Made in 1987, the pattern is a double wedding ring, the various pieces sewn by machine and then hand quilted, with a design taken from the Roman pavement at Rockbourne, Wiltshire (Accession number A.1991.234).

BLANKET

Another interesting item in the NMS collection is a twill woven wool blanket, embroidered in coloured wool threads with various motifs, including thistles, and the initials and date 'IC 1705' (Accession number A.1942.41). Embroidered blankets seem to be a peculiarly Scottish form within the British Isles and this is one of the earliest dated examples. It was presumably used as a top cover for a bed, and is made of two widths of narrow twill wool in what was probably a cream colour that has now become discoloured. It is well worn and there are many small darns where moths and wear have inflicted damage.

The blanket was given to NMS by Miss A Leslie of Dunblane, complete with the information that it had been worked by Isobel Carmichael, but with no indication of who she was and if she was related to the donor in any way. In the letters of Isabella Murray Wright, written in 1894, she records this blanket as having been worked by a daughter of her great, great grandfather, Dr George Murray, who married a Mr Carmichael in Edinburgh.[57] However, the dates for Dr Murray (1694-1749) do not fit, so it is more likely that the blanket was embroidered by one of Mr Carmichael's female relatives, possibly his sister or an aunt. As mentioned on page 57, women in Scotland did not lose their own names on marriage, so the initials may not have been his mother's or his wife's.

VALANCES

A set of embroidery done on small pieces of fabric may also have been intended for a valance. Bought at auction in 1985, the embroideries are worked in coloured silk threads on fine shot green silk backed by linen (Accession number K.2001.722). There are eleven pieces in total, each worked with two small floral motifs, above and below two letters, in yellow silk over white cord. When the panels are laid out, they spell at the top, 'Sir Coline Campbell of GK', and below, 'Dame Ieliane Campbell 1632'. These panels are unused, but it is possible they were to be applied to the valance of a bed. The names are those of Colin Campbell of Glenorchy and his wife

Opposite:
Embroidered wool blanket by Isobel Carmichael, dated 1705.
(A.1942.41)

Two details from the piece opposite.

Julian Campbell of Loudon. Colin Campbell succeeded his father in 1631 and died in 1640, so these panels reflect his new status. They may have been intended for the bed described in the Balloch inventory of 1640 as made of 'changing taffite greine and yellow', but the description of the valance does not fit these panels. Instead it may be that the long valance of cross-stitch with the arms of Sir Colin and his wife in the Metropolitan Museum of Art, New York, was used on this bed.[58]

Among the earliest household embroideries acquired by NMS (in 1858) are two valances from Iceland. Originally two separate pieces, they are now joined together (Accession number A.1858.303).[59] They were bought by NMS from R M Smith of Leith, together with various other Icelandic and Faroese pieces. The top valance is 4080mm long and 770mm wide, a loom width; the lower one is 3590mm long and 593mm wide, and is made of slightly coarser linen. The linen is natural coloured and the design is worked in straight darning or glitsaumer, counted-thread work executed from charted designs, mainly in red and blue wool threads. This stitch appears to have been very popular in Iceland. The pattern on the lower

Detail of the stitches from the lower panel of the piece above.

piece includes stylised birds in a tree, separated by a trellis of crosses through small squares. It contains an inscription which reads in translation: 'Whoever gets possession of this hanging shall never let go happiness.' The top valance has a diamond pattern, each compartment being filled with a very stylised flower design and a long inscription at the top and bottom. This is the eleventh verse from the thirty-fourth Passion Hymn of the Icelandic minister and poet Hallgrímur Pétursson (1614-74), written in 1659 and published in 1666. In direct translation the verse reads: 'At the very last when I shall here obey my death, be then, my God before thy sight thy son's heavy sufferings, when he was laid low on the tree and looked to thee with weeping eyes. Therefore, for his sake, spare me.' A poetic translation by Arthur Charles Gook, an Englishman who lived in Akureyri, northern Iceland, in the early twentieth century, reads:

> And when from earth at length I rise
> From this life's tribulation,
> My God, bring then before my eyes
> My Saviour's expiation,
> When on the cross, He prostrate lay
> And gave His life that fatal day
> To Compass my salvation!

Because of the date of the composition of this hymn, the valance cannot be any earlier than the late seventeenth century, but it is perhaps more likely to be early eighteenth century in date.

The two pieces were reputed to have hung in the tent at Thingvellir, where the Althing met until 1798, before it was moved to Reykjavik. The Althing was the Icelandic parliament, a mixture of a judicial court and a law-making institution, held every year. It had originally been a lively meeting place where the whole nation could trade, meet friends and family, as well as attend the main business of the assembly. By the seventeenth century it had become the place where the Danish king's proclamations were made public and where lawsuits were brought, judgements given and sentences carried out. Thingvellir consisted of a farm and church with several other farms in the vicinity. Although the Althing was originally held outdoors, in 1690 a stone and sod building was erected for the lögrétta, the superior court, later replaced by a wooden building in about 1750. The hangings cannot have hung in a tent, but must have been used in one of the later buildings, probably the wooden one.

The use of these embroidered valances in a building at Thingvellir must have been secondary. The long narrow pieces are similar to bed valances, like an eighteenth-century example in the National Museum of Iceland (Inv. No.1808) which is 3800mm by 510mm. The incorporation of the evening hymns was also common. The lower valance is close in design to another piece in the National Museum of Iceland – NMI 615. There were no professional embroiderers as such in Iceland, but some women did work on a semi-professional basis.

The person from whom NMS acquired these embroideries would appear to be Robert Mackay Smith, described in various *Post Office Directories* as a merchant in Leith, where he had an office from at least 1832 to 1879. In the 1881 Census he is described as a Steam Ship Owner, aged 78, born in Glasgow, unmarried and living at 4 Bellevue Crescent, Edinburgh, where he had resided for at least thirty years. Unfortunately there is no information in the directories as to what kind of merchant he was, but the acquisition from him of the Faroese and Icelandic material suggests his trading links were with Scandinavia rather than further south. Traces of the valances in Icelandic sources are equally frustrating. In the notebooks for 1858-9 of Sigurður Guðmundsson, the painter, who instigated the founding of the National Museum of Iceland in 1863, mention is made of the NMS valances. The notes read that an Englishman had obtained the hangings in 1858 and they were now in a museum of antiquities in Edinburgh. Later, c.1863-64, he mentions them again: '... in Edinburgh in a museum, is the legislative hangings, lögréttu tjadilð, from Skefing. It is entirely floral design. Jón saw it.' The name Skefing must refer to Hallgrímur Scheving (1781-1861), a teacher at the 'Learned School' at Bessastaðir, near Reyjavik. In the autobiography of Benedikt Gröndal (1826-1907), son of the headmaster of the school, he recalls seeing the tiny sitting room of Scheving's house entirely hung with old wall hangings. Presumably the NMS embroideries were among them.

Part of the lower valance – detail from the piece on pages 68-9.

EMBROIDERED PICTURES

Embroidered pictures were a feature of domestic embroidery from the late sixteenth century and NMS owns many examples of charming seventeenth-century pictures.[60] The late eighteenth century was another period when small needlework pictures, often on satin grounds, were produced. Time has not always

One of three panels from 'The Red Cross Knight' series, by Phoebe Anna Traquair, showing the knight slaying the dragon. Signed 'P.A.T.' and dated '1904'.
(A.1937.363)

been kind to these examples, but they do survive in quite large numbers and are well represented in the NMS collections.

As well as several Berlin woolwork pictures from the nineteenth century, NMS has some larger pictures dating from the early twentieth century. Three are by Phoebe Anna Traquair. They form a series called 'Una and the Red Cross Knight' based on *The Faerie Queen*, a poem by Edmund Spenser (Accession numbers A.1937.362 and 363, and A.1947.158). The pictures took many years to produce, being dated 1904, 1907 and 1914, as they are very large panels. They were intensively worked in coloured silks, framed and are glazed. Phoebe Traquair is better known for her enamel work and paintings, but there are other large embroidery series that have been created by her.

Another artist and near contemporary was Maggie Hamilton, who worked a large panel, 'Doves and Clematis', probably for her new home, Long Croft, Helensburgh, in 1902 (Accession number A.1983.1156). The house was designed by her husband Alexander N Paterson, an architect. The panel was one of several that she worked.[61]

THE PROFESSIONAL EMBROIDERER

ECCLESIASTICAL

Church embroidery from before the split with Rome in the mid-sixteenth century is rare from British sources. Churches were furnished with embroideries and woven textiles, mainly for the various altars, but there were also curtains and backcloths to the altars, and sometimes tapestries were also used. The various vestments that the officiating clergy wore could also add to the decorative scheme within a church in a way that people's clothes in a secular setting might not.

The embroidery traditions of England in the mediaeval period, known abroad as *opus anglicanum*, are preserved in many splendid vestments such as the 'Syon cope' in the Victoria & Albert Museum. NMS possesses two fragments of orphreys from this style, bought with the aid of the National Art Collections Fund (Accession number A.1956.1493 and A). There are also three examples of late-fifteenth to early-sixteenth style. This appears to have been extremely popular as many examples survive. They show the Virgin Mary ascending to heaven, surrounded by winged seraphim standing on wheels and stylised lilies, known in

Opposite:
Altar frontal of velvet with embroidered motifs — detail of the Virgin Mary with attendant angels, English, early 16th century.
(A.1964.305)

The complete piece (left).

the mediaeval period as 'Mary's flowers'. These are worked on velvet, although sometimes the figure of Mary is worked separately and applied.

The NMS pieces are altar frontals, cut from the back of copes. One of them was bought and the other two were bequeathed by Sir Archibald Buchan Hepburn (Accession numbers A.1964.305 and H.NA 509). The latter two pieces are now joined together, most likely to form a curtain for behind an altar. They are not from the same set of vestments and so probably came from different embroidery workshops. The family considers these pieces to be connected with Mary, Queen of Scots. A complete cope, with its orphreys, in this style of embroidery, is in the collection of the Art Institute of Chicago and came originally from Whallay Abbey, Lancashire. The design of these late embroideries is considered to be inferior to their earlier counterparts and they have not attracted the attention of embroidery historians.

The Fetternear Banner

The earliest surviving piece of professional embroiderers' work from a Scottish workshop is the 'Fetternear Banner', a processional banner produced c.1520 (Accession number H.LF 23).[62] Made of linen – 1500mm high by 795mm wide – the piece is worked in coloured silks in double running, or Holbein stitch, so that the design is the same on both sides. Satin stitch and split stitch are used in one or two places. The rows of stitches are staggered and worked very close together. The design consists of a central panel divided into two. The top part is vacant and there is no indication of what was intended. The lower part contains the Image of Pity, Christ in loin cloth with drops of blood all over, standing in front of a Tau cross with the sepulchre at his feet, with the Instruments of the Passion above and to the sides. Prominent above the cross are two heads, the spitting man and Judas with the purse containing the thirty pieces of silver. All round the central panel are three borders. The inner one depicts the rosary, divided into decades of five, the paternoster beads being double red roses. The middle border is a cordeliere as worn by Franciscans third orders and confraternities; and the outer border, which was never finished, was of columbines and scallop shells. There are also three coats of arms – those of the Grahams of Fintry, Gavin Douglas, Bishop of Dunkeld, and the third vacant, probably for the Archbishop of St Andrews.

Opposite:
The Fetternear Banner,
Scottish, C. 1520.
(H.LF 23)

Shield showing the arms of Christ, a dove on a red ground, the rosary border and the cordeliere border (above), *and the cock crowing* (right) – *details from the Fetternear Banner on page 77.*

The iconography suggests that this banner was made for a Confraternity of the Holy Blood and the design was probably taken from one of the many German woodcuts produced at this time. There was such a confraternity in Edinburgh, and they had built a new chapel in St Giles' church in 1518. This banner was probably intended as a gift from a prominent member or office bearer to help furnish the chapel. The arms suggest that the donor was Alexander Graham, a kirkmaister in 1522. Graham was also a furrier and burgess of Edinburgh. The Confraternity of the Holy Blood, founded in the fifteenth century, was composed of the merchant burghers of the city, but also included King James IV.

Gavin Douglas was Bishop of Dunkeld from 1515 until his death in 1522 and also Provost of St Giles. The unfinished state of the banner can probably be explained by the fact that Gavin Douglas, a prominent figure at the courts of James IV and James V, was involved in various intrigues for which he was declared a rebel in 1521. He fled to London and died there of the plague the following year. It is unlikely that anyone would have wanted to continue this banner after Douglas's death with his arms so prominent, and it may be that it was not possible to remove them and substitute others. It is also possible that the donor of the banner was involved too heavily with Douglas and wanted to take a lower profile.

The technical expertise of this piece suggests that at least one workshop in Edinburgh had attained a very high standard. It is unlikely that the piece was worked abroad, and indeed no other piece is known from anywhere at this date using the same technique.[63] The unfinished state suggests local work, where the disgrace of the bishop would be known very quickly, allowing the workshop, and the client, to urgently review matters in the light of the new information. Had it been worked outside Edinburgh, the news would have reached them too late to stop the completion of the banner.

Greek

The Greek embroideries from Epirus in the north west of the country reveal strong influences from Turkey. Epirus was part of the Ottoman Empire during the eighteenth century. The two long embroideries in the NMS collection were probably made in professional workshops. They have been described as bed valances, but their length is possibly too great for this purpose. This has led one recent writer to consider them to be altar frontals or communion rail cloths for the Roman Catholic community of the coastal towns, an area controlled by the Venetians.[64] The iconography on these pieces is not as specifically Christian as expected on Catholic embroideries, but their size copies similar pieces found in northern Italy at the same period.

Both of the NMS pieces are embroidered on two narrow widths of linen sewn together horizontally, with the top left plain where a superfrontal would have concealed it. They are over 3500mm (3.5 metres) in length and about 800mm in width. One piece has a stamp on the back, probably a customs stamp for the cloth,

Altar frontal from Parga, Epirus, Greece, 18th century. (A.1946.62)

but it is difficult to read as the embroidery obscures it. The embroidery is worked in coloured silk threads in split, chain, double running and cross-stitches.

One frontal, given by Miss Janie Allan, is described as coming from Parga, one of the coastal towns (Accession number A.1946.62). It has a repeating design of stylised winged angels separated by vases of tulips. There are four angels with green faces and red tufted hair. The top of each body is red with a blue skirt decorated with a stylised bird. The wings are green, with green and red long feathers. Birds, flowers and animals surround each figure. The outer panel on the left is probably missing, but the one on the right includes birds and flowers, making six compartments in total along the length. Between these are broad panels of stylised flowers, all identical. Below the figures is a wonderful border full of figures and flowers. At the right is a castle and on the left a ship, with a unicorn, lion, dancing women, riders, birds and many small figures, flowers and animals in between.

The other embroidery is probably complete and was bequeathed by Mrs Zoë Manuel, a member of the Ionides family (A.1974.141). It is divided into five main compartments, each one different, and separated by narrow panels, the two either side of the centre being virtually the same as those on the other piece. The central panel is a man in Ottoman dress on horseback, with a ship above, and surrounded by figures, flowers, birds and animals. To the right the next panel has a castle, with guards and prisoners, a large vase of flowers below, and two women dancing. The narrow panel shows two vases of flowers and a deer. The last large panel on the right has a stylised tulip and two peacocks, with the narrow end panel consisting of a deer and eagle. To the left of the central panel is a tulip in a pot with other flowers in vases. The vase and deer narrow panel is then repeated. The last large panel has a vase of flowers and a man and woman on

Altar frontal from Epirus, Greece, 18th century. (A.1974.141)

either side. Above this are ewers and horsemen. The end panel repeats the deer and eagle motif. Along the bottom is a small border with a repeating motif of men on horses and a cypress tree. On three sides there is a fringe of red, green, blue white and pale orange. Red is a prominent colour on both these textiles, the other main colours being green and blue, reminiscent of the colours of Isnik tiles produced in Turkey.

Horseman in Ottoman style dress – detail from the piece opposite.

These two pieces are the most outstanding of the NMS Greek embroidery collection. They are interesting and important because of their completeness. Too often embroideries of this length have been cut up, either for re-use during their lifetime, or by dealers who could get more money by selling the panels separately. The size of these altar or communion rail cloths must have hindered their interest to collectors, many of whom use their collections to decorate their own homes.

After the Reformation (late sixteenth century), church vestments were not regularly used in Britain until the Victorian period, despite the attempts of Archbishop Laud and King Charles I in the 1630s to reintroduce them. NMS's collection of later church furnishings is mostly vestments including copes, chasubles and mitres of continental origin, as well as many fragments of silks cut from vestments. One particularly fine cope is made of a green woven silk in a style of pattern known as 'Bizarre' from the rather exotic designs that were a feature of silks in the early years of the eighteenth century (Accession number A.1983.792). The fabric could equally well have been made into a woman's dress, and many vestments for both Roman Catholic churches and Jewish synagogues at this period were made from gowns donated by worshippers. Modern church ceremonial has given scope for both the embroiderer and the hand weaver to create new vestments, and NMS owns a cope made by the weaver Hilda Breed (Accession number A.1980.1003). This reflects the desire for vestments that are lighter in weight than Victorian pieces, which were often made of very heavy materials and sometimes lined and interlined to create a stiff, rather unyielding shape, with heavy metal fastenings.

Edmund Harrison

Little is known about the professional embroidery workshops in Britain in the seventeenth and eighteenth centuries. The records of the Broderers' Company in London were destroyed in the Great Fire in 1666, but in the Royal Wardrobe accounts of England for the early seventeenth century, something of the secular work that was still carried out by professional embroiderers can be seen. This is of particular interest because NMS owns two of a set of six embroideries, three of them being inscribed on the back with the name of the King's Embroiderer 'Edmund Harrison' as the maker, and the date '1637'. The life and career of Edmund Harrison have been painstakingly traced to give us some idea of what kind of work such a professional undertook in an age largely devoid of church commissions.[65] Information on the physical operation of an embroidery workshop is given in some French publications, such as the book by Charles Germain de Saint-Aubin, embroiderer to the French King, Louis XV. *L'Art du Brodeur* was published in 1770.[66]

Edmund Harrison (1590-1667) was the grandson of a Lancashire country gentleman whose son became a merchant tailor in London and married the daughter of a Yorkshireman in 1580. Edmund was therefore born into a family of minor country gentry who established themselves as city merchants. He went to the Merchant Taylors' school in London, leaving in 1604 when he presumably started an apprenticeship to an embroiderer, which in London appears to have lasted for eight years. He was in partnership with John Shepley as King's Embroiderer by 1621 under James I, but the new king, Charles I, granted Harrison the exclusive right to that office when he succeeded in 1625. Harrison rose up the ranks of the Broderers' Company becoming Warden in 1628, and held a public office as a churchwarden of St Benet's, Paul's Wharf, a post that carried a considerable burden during this period. In 1630 Harrison married Jane, the daughter of Thomas Godfrey, a neighbour and friend in Grub Street, who had moved out to Kent. Jane was the sister of the unfortunate Sir Edmund Berry Godfrey, murdered in 1678 at the time of the Popish Plot, a plot devised by Titus

'The Visitation',
from the series of 'The
Life of the Virgin', by
Edmund Harrison, 1637.
(A.1963.62)

Oates and others in 1678-9 in which they alleged that Roman Catholics were planning to murder King Charles II. Berry Godfrey was the magistrate to whom Oates took his information on the 'supposed' plot and Edmund Harrison was one of Sir Edmund's godfathers. During the Commonwealth period in the 1650s, when there was likely to be little for a professional embroiderer to do, Edmund Harrison appears to have entered the coal trade, a highly lucrative market in London. By the time Charles II was restored to the throne in 1660, Edmund Harrison was seventy years old, but he retained his position as King's Embroiderer until his death seven years later.

From the Great Wardrobe accounts it is possible to detail the kind of work that such a professional embroiderer's workshop undertook. In effect, the King's Embroiderer, part of the king's household, was the major embroiderer in the

Opposite:
'The Circumcision'
from the series 'The Life
of the Virgin', by
Edmund Harrison, 1637.
(A.1984.317)

country, supplying all the rich liveries required by the court: cloths of state, heralds' tabards, chancellors' purses, trumpet banners, saddle cloths and horse trappers, and even covers for the wagons used to convey the king's hunting hounds. This was in addition to work on the personal clothing of the king and domestic household items such as table covers and bed hangings.

The major period of Edmund Harrison's work covered the reign of Charles I in the 1620s and 30s. The kind of official items he supplied can be seen from other items in NMS's collection. A heraldic piece, known as the Hay Banner, was supposed to have been the one carried at the battle of Worcester in 1651 by a member of the Hay family (Accession number H.RHB6).[67] The arms, however, are those of James VI as king of Scotland, with a unicorn and thistle on the left and a lion and rose on the right. The piece, which is very worn and faded, is more likely to be the back panel for a throne. It could have been made for the one and only visit of James to Scotland in 1617 after he inherited the English throne. Very elaborate preparations were made for this visit, but unfortunately there are no records of who might have worked this piece.

Another Royal coat of arms in the NMS collection is reputedly from the Council Chambers in Edinburgh (Accession number H.RHB6). The arms are probably those of Charles II, and they may well be the arms that Robert Porteous was commissioned to work for the Session House in Edinburgh.[68] A further piece that may be related is a trumpet banner with the Scottish Royal Arms and Charles II's cipher (Accession number A.1988.187). Patricia Wardle has found no evidence that these Scottish examples were worked in London, although heraldic pieces for Ireland are mentioned. This suggests that the NMS banner was worked in Edinburgh. Against this must be set the fact that a similar piece with the English Royal Arms exists from the same source.

Another official piece is the herald's tabard with the Scottish Royal Arms of Queen Anne, as used from 1702 to 1707 before the Union of the Parliaments of England and Scotland. This is also in the NMS collection, and might have been worked in Edinburgh (Accession number A.1888.303). When it was conserved it showed the work of two different hands, possibly representing two embroiderers in the same workshop, or two different workshops. Both of these types of embroideries, trumpet banners and heralds' tabards, can be seen in use in the print of the Riding

to Parliament in Edinburgh dated to 1680-5, and indicate that although the Court had moved south in 1603 there was still some official work for the state in Scotland, at least until the Union of the Parliaments in 1707.

The definite Harrison pieces in the NMS collection are two embroideries from a set of the 'Life of the Virgin'. The set, as it survived to the 1920s, consisted of six pieces, three small and three larger, with three being inscribed and dated in ink on the back: 'Edmund Harrison Imbroderer to King Charles m[ade this] 1637.' The three dated pieces are in the Victoria & Albert Museum, which has 'The Adoration of the Shepherds' (Accession number T.147-1930), the Fitzwilliam Museum, which has 'The Marriage of the Virgin' (Accession number T.1-1965), the same size as the NMS piece, and NMS, which has 'The Visitation' (Accession number A.1963.61). In addition, NMS bought one of the other unsigned larger pieces, 'The Circumcision' (Accession number A.1984.317). The current whereabouts of two pieces are unknown: 'The Adoration of the Magi' and 'The Annunciation'.

What sets these pieces apart from the rest of the British embroideries of the seventeenth century is the fact that they are worked in *or nué*, a style of embroidery favoured on continental work for church embroidery. It was perfected there by the

Herald's tabard with the Royal Arms as borne in Scotland, 1702-7. (A.1888.303)

The reverse of 'The Visitation' to show the inscription. (A.1963.62, see page 85)

Detail showing the two types of embroidery — or nué and silk threads — used on the pieces illustrated on pages 84 and 85.

mid-fifteenth century when the stunning set of vestments for the Order of the Golden Fleece, now in Vienna, was made.[69] The technique is described by St Aubin.[70] Basically the ground is made of gold threads laid either horizontally or vertically, the details being worked in coloured silk threads over the gold. This gives a very rich depth to the work and naturally costs a great deal with so much gold thread. To create the best effect, the embroiderer needed a good supply of silk threads in many hues to make the subtle shading that the technique could achieve. St Aubin suggests that twenty threaded needles were needed at any one time. The embroiderer also required a good design, which was drawn on the cloth first, and the embroiderer had to push the gold threads aside to see the outline and to judge where to put the various colours. The source of Harrison's 'Life of the Virgin' series is not known, but the scenes were probably not from one set of prints. A possible source has been suggested for 'The Visitation': that of an engraving of 1593 by Hendrick Goltzius. The whole set also shows the influence of the Counter Reformation on Catholic iconography. Harrison would have had the designs drawn onto the cloth for him, and there are several possible people within the Royal circle who could have done this, including Wenceslaus Hollar and Peter Oliver.

When the embroideries were sold in 1922 they had entered the collection of Henry Howard of Corby Castle, near Carlisle, with the information that they had been in the possession of William Howard, Lord Stafford, and at Corby since the mid-seventeenth century. However, Corby Castle belonged to a different branch of the family. Subsequent research showed that they had in fact been given to Henry Howard by the eleventh Duke of Norfolk. Patricia Wardle, in her article, suggests that the commissioner of this set of embroideries could have been Lady Alethea Talbot, wife of Thomas, Earl of Arundel and a grand daughter of Bess of Hardwick. Lady Arundel was a Catholic, and in 1637 her son, William Howard, married Mary, the sister and heiress of her brother, Lord Stafford, who died just before this marriage. William Howard then took the title Lord Stafford. It is possible that Lady Arundel had the embroideries made as a wedding present for her son, or for her house at Tart Hall, London, where she may have had a chapel.

'The Visitation' (Luke 1: 39-56) shows the Virgin at the left visiting her cousin Elisabeth (right), with Zacharias, Elisabeth's husband, behind them in his priest's robes. Her companion is possibly Mary Cleophas or Mary Salome. The picture is now in a contemporary mid seventeenth-century tortoiseshell frame. The back of the embroidery is inscribed in ink (see page 87). It was bought from the London dealer, Mayorcas, in 1922, but its whereabouts between then and its acquisition by NMS are unknown.

'The Circumcision' (Luke 2: 2-21) shows the priest wielding the knife over Jesus, who is held by an older woman, possibly Elisabeth, with Joseph behind her. Mary may be the figure on the far right. Behind the priest are two figures more properly associated with the presentation in the Temple. Simeon is on the left, singing his song of praise: 'Lord now lettest thou thy servant depart in peace.'[71] To the right is Anna, the prophetess, with two children holding candles. This embroidery has had a piece cut out of it at the lower right, possibly to repair one of the missing embroideries if it were damaged, or to make it fit a particular space. It was bought from Spink and Son, and its whereabouts between 1922 and 1981 are unknown.

These two embroideries, although from the same series, are from different pictorial sources. 'The Visitation' is a rather naïve rendering in its composition, whilst 'The Circumcision' shows greater subtlety in the composition and in the working of the threads. The shading of the marble floor and garments is much more lively than the more static 'Visitation' with its stylised clouds and garment folds. Of the other two pieces that can still be seen, 'The Marriage of the Virgin' shares the same rather static pose as 'The Visitation', while 'The Adoration of the Shepherds' is closer to 'The Circumcision'. Why only three of the six pieces have been attributed to Edmund Harrison by the inscription on the back is unclear. Possibly he did work on the embroidery on these pieces, but as King's Embroiderer he must have had a fairly busy administrative life that cannot have left much time to do any actual embroidery. It is unlikely that he actually signed the pieces.

DOMESTIC EMBROIDERIES

Lochleven and Linlithgow hangings

The so-called 'Lochleven' and 'Linlithgow' hangings were produced in a professional embroidery workshop.[72] NMS has owned one panel and two valances of the 'Lochleven' set since 1921 when the National Art Collections Fund helped the Royal Scottish Museum to acquire it (Accession number A.1921.68 A and B). The rest were bought by Lord Bute and eventually acquired by the Burrell Collection in 1996. The Linlithgow hanging was acquired in 1931 (Accession number A.1931.34).

Motif from the Lochleven hangings, late 16th or early 17th century. (A.1921.68)

Two other panels are known, now at St Leonard's School, St Andrews. They were thought to have been worked by Mary, Queen of Scots, but there is no evidence to prove this. Both were probably wall hangings, although they have had some alterations over the last 400 years. They were embroidered in yellow silk and appliqué black velvet on a red wool ground resembling velvet when new, but now much worn. Originally the sets must have looked very rich, with the yellow silk being a cheaper substitute for gold. The design is of vertical border bands down each side, and one or more down the centre, with a band along the lower edge, and individual motifs between the bands. Although the two sets are worked in the same way, the Lochleven set is the more finely embroidered. They were probably made in the late sixteenth or early years of the seventeenth century at a workshop in Edinburgh.

James VI, before he moved to London on inheriting the English crown in 1603 (becoming James I), would have required similar kinds of embroidery to those Edmund Harrison was later to produce for him in London. William Beatoun, who died in 1620, was Embroiderer to the King in Edinburgh. Evidence of other embroiderers from this period suggests there were professionals in Scotland who could have made these sets.

Valances

Valances usually matched the curtains or hangings they covered, but there are some that appear to be unrelated to any curtains or hangings. These are usually found in sets of three, one shorter than the others. This suggests that they were used on the tops of beds, or just possibly for the edges of cloths of estate that were placed over the chairs of the wealthy house owner. They are almost certainly the work of professional embroiderers.

Two of the embroidered valances in NMS date to the 1580s and come from Murthley Castle, Perthshire. They were in the Noel Paton collection (Accession number A.1905. 1022 and 1023). The subject matter on these pieces was thought to depict Queen Elizabeth I, but one is in fact the story of Esther and Ahasureus (Book of Esther). They are now rather faded and have suffered cuts and repairs in the past.

The panels belong to a group of valances that are often described as Franco-Scottish, because several pieces have been found in Scottish houses and are usually worked in petit point on canvas.[73] The scenes on them, like the tapestries, are from the Bible or mythology, and their subject matter is sometimes obscure to today's audience. The other distinguishing feature is that the people are depicted wearing French court dress of the time of Henri III, *ie* the 1580s. Despite this, the prevailing view is that some were probably made in Britain, but where and by whom is not clear. Most sets have come from houses within the British Isles, though the source of one set recently on the market was a French château. There are several examples in the Untermyer collection in New York[74], and others in the Lady Lever Art Gallery[75], as well as in other museum collections. Very few have any real provenance, as most were bought from dealers at a time when people were less concerned about evidence of origin for textiles.

NMS also owns a set of valances known as the 'Morton' valances (Accession number A.1988.139 A-C). These were acquired in 1973 from Lord Glentanner, but originally came from the collection of the Earls of Morton.[76] Unfortunately this set is incomplete, because by extraordinary coincidence two groups of similar valances have become mixed up in the past. As far as known, there is no good explanation as to how this mix-up could have happened if the panels had been in their respective collections since they were made. The NMS set has two valances

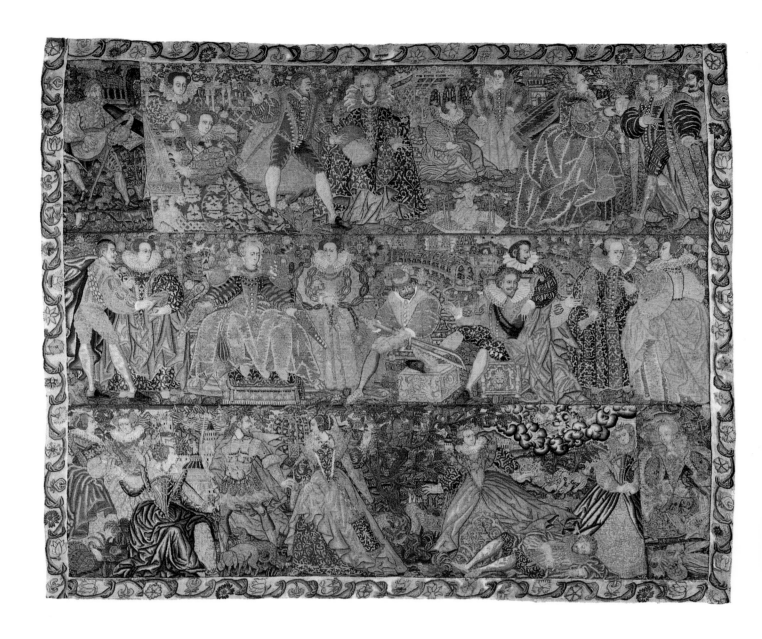

The three Morton valances showing their present appearance. The top and bottom are shorter than the central valance and have been extended with fragments from other valances.
(A. 1988. 139)

showing scenes from an unknown story, which includes a man having his foot cut off and being very stoical about it! The third piece is the story of the death of Orion by Artemnis, and belongs to a set owned by Lord Forbes. The episode featured comes from the story of Leto and Artemis, as found in Ovid's *Metamorphoses*. Other scenes from the tale are shown on two of the Forbes panels. His third panel belongs to NMS's set.[77] In addition, to make up the panel size to which all three of the museum's valances are now sewn, odd scraps from other panels of embroidery have been added that show people wearing clothes of a slightly earlier date. A border of trailing flowers has been added from another embroidery.

Both the Morton and Forbes valances have been attributed to Mary, Queen of Scots and her ladies, but as Margaret Swain has shown Mary could not have had time to work all the pieces she is credited with.[78] A more serious consideration in this case is the style of clothing worn by the richly-dressed people, which can date the panels. They are wearing very elaborate garments with the brocade patterns of the woven silks and velvets meticulously embroidered on the canvas. However, the colours have faded and it is not always possible to see details clearly. In the lower panel, and in the Forbes pieces, the women's sleeves are full, but have pronounced rolls at the top, similar to those worn in the portrait of an unknown woman, 1575-80, in the National Portrait Gallery, London[79] and originally thought to be of Mary, Queen of Scots. In the two top panels the men and women are dressed with large, full sleeves, with long pointed waists to their doublets and gowns. The women's clothes echo those worn by Queen Elizabeth in the Armada portrait of 1588-9.[80] In all these panels many of the women have muffs hanging from their waists on chains or ribbons. Made of brocade with fur edgings, muffs were a new and obviously very fashionable accessory in this period. One of the small added pieces shows a woman with a muff on which there are several letters, all doubled – 'MФDV'. They do not appear to make much sense.[81] Both men and women in the top Morton panels are wearing backless slippers over their shoes.

A woman in elaborate clothes and with a muff hanging from her waist – detail from the bottom valance of the piece opposite.

A man having his foot cut off – detail from the central valance of the piece shown opposite.

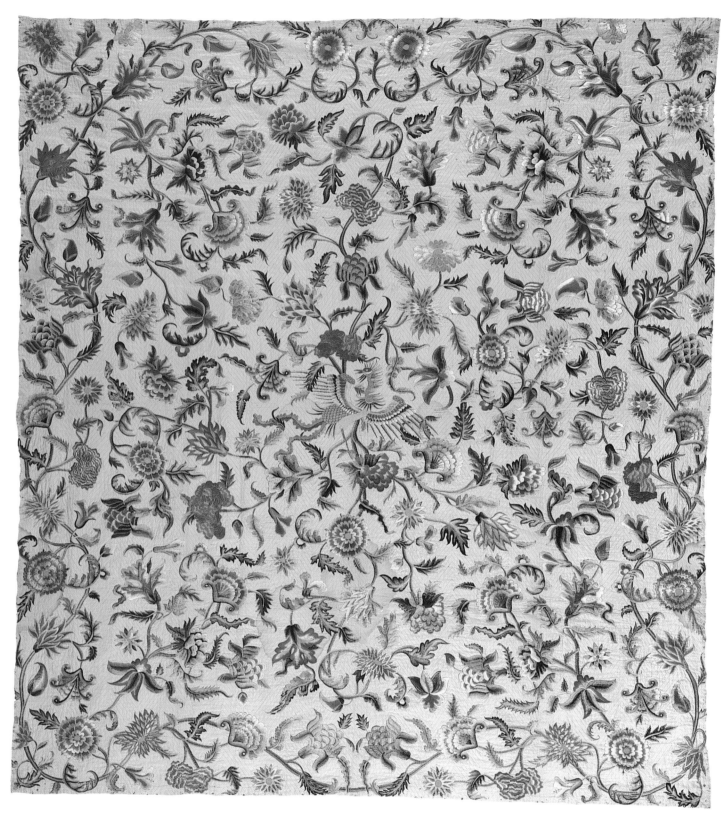

*Embroidered bed cover
with exotic bird and
flower design.*
(A.1956.1302)

The figures on these panels are often shown against a background of beautiful gardens, as in these sets, and reflect the court culture of France in the late sixteenth century. The quality of the needlework technique is very high, suggesting a professional workshop. The Earls of Morton and the family of Lord Forbes both have links to Mary, Queen of Scots, and it may be that they retained a connection with France after her abdication that would have made them sympathetic to the acquisition of such embroideries. Against this must the set the fact that nothing is known of the history of the panels before they were found in the nineteenth century in the houses of the two families. The mix-up of the two sets might well indicate that they were in the hands of dealers who, when they came to present them for sale, inadvertently swapped them over.

Quilted bed covers

The earliest style of quilted bed cover now represented in the collection is a type that might be termed 'false quilting', because there is no padding between the two layers of fabric.[82] It was a form of bed covering popular in the first half of the eighteenth century when elaborate quilts were embroidered, together with matching bolster and pillow covers. The covers would be removed at night, and it is possible that the bed covers were also taken off to protect such expensive items from damage. These quilts were often made of satin, with a highly decorative design on the top sewn in coloured silk threads, sometimes with touches of gold. The ground was then worked all over with closely spaced back-stitched lines in yellow silk in zig-zags, meanders, diamonds or scallops. The backing fabric is usually coarse linen and original examples were often lined in silk. There are references to them being given as wedding presents. One example, now in the Victoria & Albert Museum[83], was presented to the Rev. John Dolbin and his wife in 1717. Mrs Dolbin was a sister of Lord Digby. Another quilt at Longleat House, near Bath, was given to Lady Louisa Carteret when she married the second Viscount Weymouth. It dates from 1733.

One part cover in the NMS collection has been cut down to form a panel that is now 1780mm by 1580mm, and appears to have been framed for hanging on the wall (Accession number A.1956.1302). It is embroidered with an exotic bird in the centre, surrounded by equally exotic flowers and leaves worked in long and short stitches, with French knots in the centre of the flowers. The background has zig-

Detail from the piece opposite.

Opposite:
*Embroidered bed cover
with monograms and
figures in Turkish
style dress
(A.1927.270)*

*Details from the
same piece.*

zags in yellow silk that have first been marked on the ground in black. As it has never been washed, these black lines give a rather dark look to the yellow zig-zags. This particular piece was bought from the estate of Mabell, Dowager Countess of Airlie, but it is not known if she found it in her Scottish home, Cortachy Castle, or inherited it from her own family, the Gores, Earls of Arran.[84] Mabell Airlie was a friend and lady-in-waiting to Queen Mary, but she was apparently no needlewoman. Queen Mary was patron of the Royal School of Needlework in London, which appears to have repaired and sold old embroideries, and NMS bought several pieces from the School. It is just possible that Lady Airlie also acquired this piece from them.

From the Needlework Development Scheme, NMS acquired another linen ground quilt, complete this time, with its sides and the background embroidered in close lines both ways to form small diamond shapes, also back stitched in yellow silk (Accession number A.1962.1055). The main design is much lighter with a central medallion, an oval medallion in each corner, a border of floral sprays and small sprays scattered over the ground, mainly in red and green silks in chain, satin, back and buttonhole wheel stitches. The medallions contain Oriental style figures. In the centre there is a man with a parasol and a couple together with a pelican[?], trees with a cockerel in the branches, a person in a horse-drawn carriage, and a castle, all surrounded by a circle of flower sprays. The castle and carriage appear in each corner medallion together with trees. The corners have been shaped to fit round the foot posts of a bed, and the size is 2585mm long by 2290mm wide.

NMS has another large quilt, 2190mm by 2160mm, showing the Oriental taste so popular in the early eighteenth century, which sits rather oddly with the more typical European style of around 1700 worked on the top of the bed cover (Accession number A.1927.270). The quilt has a large monogram, bearing the letters 'M', 'G' and 'B' in the style used by William III and Queen Mary for their double monogram, but it is difficult to know in which order the letters should be placed. This monogram is repeated in each corner, while the rest of the area is covered by a balanced design of strapwork, enclosing curved compartments and a wreath of leaves around each monogram. An edging border consists of daisy-like flower heads in different colourways. The sides and bottom, which fall over the sides of the bed, contain three rows of figures and birds. The figures are wearing clothing reminiscent of Persian or Turkish styles.

A much more elaborate quilt in the collection comes from Germany. It is of blue silk, embroidered in coloured and applied silks, with large flower sprays and a central medallion of a wreath surrounding coats of arms on pedestals (Accession number A.1962.509). The left pedestal has the initials 'CLvM', the right one 'HvB', with the date '1738' in between. The edge is sewn in yellow silk to imitate gold lace. The background is quilted in a simple diamond pattern, backed by pink linen and edged with pink silk braid. The coats of arms are those of the von Mansbach and von Budtlar families, and it was probably created to commemorate a marriage between the two families. This is a more elaborate quilt than any of the British examples and was probably part of a formal bed set. The white linen embroidered quilts would appear to be more in keeping with everyday bedding, as they could probably all have been washable when originally made. However, these elaborately embroidered quilts would never have been washed.

END NOTE

THE use of embroidered textiles as a major part of the decorative scheme for the home probably reached its peak in Britain in the late seventeenth and early eighteenth centuries. They were then replaced by wallpaper and woven fabric on walls, and woven and printed fabrics on beds and as curtains. Embroidery was then relegated to minor items such as cushions, fire screens, pictures and various mats, until by the 1960s it was no longer fashionable to have any items of this nature in the domestic interior.

Since the 1960s old and new embroideries have enjoyed a comeback, although limited in comparison to the richness and warmth of a seventeenth century home. Today favourite styles of embroidery include wall hangings, pictures 'painted' by needle, appliqué or collage. This is a long way from the decoration of domestic furnishings that are the subject of this book and the exhibition that inspired it.

In the past it would have been considered a waste to merely embroider a panel as a picture when the work could have been better applied to a suitable purpose. It is perhaps a measure of our contempt for useful work that we consider the modern wall hanging, an expression of the embroiderer's artistic sense and technical expertise, to be superior to these older pieces. The latter were worked with no less commitment, care, artistic merit and technical skill, not as pieces of art, but rather as useful works for the home.

Each age adjusts the inheritance it receives to suit its own ways and so embroidery has adapted over each generation. In the process it has kept alive the skills developed over millennia. If the pieces preserved in NMS can inspire a new generation to continue adapting and preserving this inheritance, then the memories of the unknown workers of these embroideries will be venerated and their labours will not have been in vain

Opposite:
Woman with a bird on her hand; detail from the Morton valances, 1580s-90s (A. 1988. 139)

NOTES

1 Quye and Williamson, 1999.
2 Stevenson, 1981.
3 Royal Scottish Museum, 1954.
4 Bennett, 1975.
5 Taylor, 1998.
6 Oddy, 1965.
7 Scottish Development Agency, c.1987.
8 Starkey, 1998.
9 Levey, 1998.
10 Margaret Maran conserved the tapestry and, together with Dr Ian Rolfe, Keeper of Geology, did the research on the piece. Their reports are in the NMS files. The complete tapestry is known only from an old photograph and its present whereabouts are unknown.
11 Scottish Arts Council, 1980. Unfortunately the Edinburgh Tapestry Company closed at the end of 2000.
12 Weavers Workshop *Newsletters*.
13 Bessborough, 1950.
14 Tarrant, 1999.
15 Sherrill, 1996, p 131.
16 The technical details of the carpet are as follows. Size: 5180mm (17ft) by 2400mm (7ft 11ins). Warps and wefts are of hemp, both Z2S dark ivory, with one shoot of weft after each row of knots. The pile is of wool Z4/5, 5mm high with a symmetrical knot, pull to left, no depression, 30H x 31V = 930kn/dm², (7 knots per inch horizontally and 8 per inch vertically). Handle, velour, very heavy, slightly floppy, smooth upper and lower ends. In the selvedge the wefts pass in and out of 10 warps with an extra binding of dark brown wool woven in and out of the 10 warps. The colours are red (ground and cartouches), orange, gold, yellow, pale yellow, light blue, light turquoise, stone, very light green, light green (outlines), dark brown (corroded), ivory. (*Hali*, volume 2, no 4, 1980, p347)
   There are four different kinds of wool represented in the pile, fine,

semi-fine, hairy-medium and generalised-medium, which equates to the range of fleece types, found in Britain. (M L Ryder, correspondence, 1991)
17 Quye, lecture.
18 Sothebys auction catalogue, 17 April 1980, lot 149. However, a reference was found by the archivist in the Glamis archives for the mending of Earl John's carpet on 26 August 1891, which almost certainly refers to this carpet.
19 Gordon Slade, 2000, pp 28-35.
20 Millar, 1890.
21 Slade, 2000, pp 52-66.
22 Gilbert, *et al*, 1987, p 89-91.
23 Parker, 1984.
24 Burnett and Bennett, 1987.
25 Nevinson, 1936, Paludan, 1991 and Wells Cole, 1997.
26 Nevinson, 1936.
27 Parker, 1984, p 106.
28 Parker, 1984, p 110.
29 Nicholas Harris Nicolas: *Privy Purse Expenses of Elizabeth of York*, 1830, reprinted 1972, p 30.
30 Clabburn, 1998, p 7.
31 Colby, 1964.
32 Tarrant, 1979, p 14.
33 Mayhew, 1986, p ii.
34 Marshall, 2000, p 252.
35 Harris, 1998.
36 C Browne, personal communication.
37 Seligman and Hughes, 1926, plate 40, for similar bead lattice on a purse.
38 Seligman and Hughes, 1926, plate 58.
39 Seligman and Hughes, 1926, plate xx.
40 Swain, 1973.
41 Bennett, 1975.
42 Accession number T.165-1930 (see Edwards, 1975, p 73).
43 Edwards, 1975, p 70.
44 Accession number T.21-1926 (see Edwards, 1975, p 81).
45 Bennett, 1975.
46 Illustrated in N Patullo: *Castles,*

Houses and Gardens of Scotland, 1967, p 120, on a canopied bed with curtains, pelmets and valances worked by Anne Smith, wife of Brigadier Grant. Anne Smith was a Maid of Honour to Queen Anne. These were also in crewelwork, but not to the same design, suggesting the original cover had either been destroyed or had not matched the curtains, and they were not sold with the bedcover in 1975. It is not known from where the bedspread panel originally came.
47 Irwin and Brett, 1970, p 67.
48 Accession number 29/241 (see Arthur, 1995, p 42).
49 Glen, 1994, p 92-3.
50 Sedgewick, 1970.
51 Tayler, 1946, p 265.
52 Ibid, p.252
53 Accession number T.2-1955.
54 V & A Accession number T.86-1928 and T.159-1975; Cardiff Accession number 54.177.1.
55 Y Cymmodorion, 1959, p 1101.
56 Osler, 1987, p 93, plate 48.
57 Wright, 1998, p 22. The date 1705 is the one traditionally given in both Wright and the NMS register. However, on the blanket it would appear that 1706 might be more correct.
58 Swain, 1986, p 27.
59 The information for this piece is based on unpublished research by Elsa E Guðjónsson, formerly Curator of Textiles in the National Museum of Iceland, Reykjavik, and the author is grateful to Mrs Guðjónsson for allowing use of her notes, a copy of which are in NMS files. Her book, *Traditional Icelandic Embroidery*, 1982, provides an introduction to the techniques and background history of embroidery in the island. The reference to Gook's translation was kindly supplied by Dr Svanhildur Óskarsdóttir, who is preparing the works of Pétursson for publication.

60 Mayhew, 1986.
61 Swain, 1986, pp 158-62.
62 MacRoberts, 1956.
63 Oddy, 1983.
64 Taylor, 1998, pp 138-40. Conservation of the pieces has revealed drops of wax on them, which would tend to confirm their identification as altar frontals.
65 See Wardle, 1994 and 1995, for the whole of this section.
66 Saint-Aubin, 1983.
67 Henshall and Maxwell, pp 284-9.
68 Ibid, p 289-90.
69 Staniland, p 44-5.
70 Saint-Aubin, p 31-2.
71 St Luke 2: 29-32.
72 Swain, 1994.
73 Scott-Moncrieff, 1917 and 1918.
74 Hackenbroch, 1960, plates 13, 16, 22.
75 Brooke, 1992, pp 203-6.
76 Bennett, 1975.
77 Illustrated in Symonds and Preece, 1928, plate liii.
78 Swain, 1973.
79 Arnold, 1988, p 153.
80 Arnold, 1988, p 35.
81 Scott-Moncrieff, 1918.
82 Colby, 1972, p 105, describes this technique as flat quilting.
83 Wardle, 1970, plate 59.
84 Ellis, 1962.

BIBLIOGRAPHY

ARNOLD, Janet: *Queen Elizabeth's Wardrobe Unlock'd* (Leeds: W S Maney & Son Ltd, 1988).

ARTHUR, Liz: *Embroidery 1600-1700 at the Burrell Collection* (London: John Murray, 1995).

BENNETT, Helen: 'Three Scottish embroideries' in *Proceedings of the Society of Antiquaries of Scotland*, 107 (1975-6), pp 330-2.

BESSBOROUGH, Earl of: *The Journal of Lady Charlotte Guest* (London: John Murray, 1950).

BROOKE, Xanthe: *The Lady Lever Art Gallery: Catalogue of Embroideries* (Stroud: Alan Sutton, 1992).

BURBIDGE, Pauline: *Quilt Studio* (Lincolnwood: Quilt Digest Press, 2000).

BURNETT, Charles J and Helen Bennett: *The Green Mantle. A Celebration of the Revival in 1687 of the Most Ancient and Most Noble Order of the Thistle* (Edinburgh: National Museums of Scotland, 1987).

CHRISTIES, South Kensington: 'An Important Collection of Needlework' [Sir Frederick Richmond] (23 June 1987) (auction catalogue).

CLABBURN, Pamela: *Samplers* (Princes Risborough: Shire) (second edition, 1998).

COLBY, Avril: *Samplers* (London: BT Batsford, 1964).

COLBY, Avril: *Quilting* (London: BT Batsford, 1972).

CYMMRODORION, Hon. Soc. Y: *The Dictionary of Welsh Biography* (Hon. Soc. Y Cymmrodorion, 1959).

ELLIS, Jennifer (ed): *Thatched with Gold: The memoirs of Mabell, Countess of Airlie* (London: Hutchinson, 1962).

EDWARDS, Joan: *Crewel Embroidery in England* (London: B T Batsford, 1975).

GILBERT, Christopher, James Lomax and Anthony Wells-Cole: *Country House Floors, 1660-1850* (Leeds: Leeds City Art Galleries, 1987).

GINSBURG, Cara and Donna Ghelerter (Introduction): *A Book of Flowers, Fruits, Beasts and Flies: Seventeenth Century Patterns for Embroiderers, printed and sold by Peter Stent* (Austin: Curious Works Press, 1995).

GLEN, Thomas L: 'Van Dyck's Rest on the Flight into Egypt' in *Gazette des Beaux-Arts*, CXXIII (1994), pp 92-3.

GUÐJÓNSSON, Elsa E: *Traditional Icelandic Embroidery* (Reykjavik: Iceland Review, 1982).

HACKENBROCH, Yvonne: *English and other Needlework, Tapestries and Textiles in the Irwin Untermyer Collection* (London: Thames & Hudson, 1960).

HARRIS, Jennifer: *A closer look at Hannah Smith's casket* (Manchester: Whitworth Art Gallery, 1998).

HENSHALL, Audrey and Stuart Maxwell: 'Two Seventeenth Century Embroidered Royal Coats of Arms' in *Proceedings of the Society of Antiquaries of Scotland*, XCV (1961-2), pp 284-90.

IRWIN, John and Katherine B Brett: *The Origins of Chintz* (London: HMSO, 1970).

LEVEY, Santina M: *An Elizabethan Inheritance: The Hardwick Hall Textiles* (London: The National Trust, 1998).

MACROBERTS, Rev David: 'The Fetternear Banner' in *The Innes Review*, 7/2 (1956), pp 69-86.

MARSHALL, Rosalind K: *The Days of Duchess Anne: Life in the Household of the Duchess of Hamilton 1656-1716* (Edinburgh: Tuckwell Press) (second edition 2000).

MAYHEW, Charlotte E J: 'The Effects of Economic and Social Developments in the Seventeenth Century, upon British Amateur Embroideries, with Particular Reference to the Collection of the National Museums of Scotland' (St Andrews: MLitt Thesis, 1986).

MILLAR, A H (editor): *The Book of Record: a diary written by*

Patrick, First Earl of Strathmore (Edinburgh: Scottish History Society, 1890).

NEVINSON, John L, Peter Stent and John Overton: 'Publishers of Embroidery Designs' in *Apollo*, XXIV (1936), pp 279-83.

ODDY, Revel: *Embroideries from Needlework Development* Scheme (Edinburgh: Royal Scottish Museum, 1965).

ODDY, Revel: 'The Fetternear Banner' in A O'Connor and D V Clarke (eds): *From the Stone Age to the 'Forty Five: Studies presented to R K B Stevenson* (Edinburgh: John Donald, 1983).

OSLER, Dorothy: *Traditional British Quilts* (London: B T Batsford, 1987).

PALUDAN, Charlotte and Lone de Hemmer Egeberg: *98 Mønster-bøger: Til Broderi, Knipling og Strikning* (Copenhagen: Det Danske Kunstindustrimuseum, 1991), in Danish and English.

PARKER, Rosika: *The Subversive Stitch: Embroidery and the making of the Feminine* (London: The Women's Press, 1984).

QUYE, Anita and Colin Williamson (eds): *Plastics, Conserving and Collecting* (Edinburgh: National Museums of Scotland Publishing, 1999).

ROYAL SCOTTISH MUSEUM: *The Royal Scottish Museum 1854-1954* (Edinburgh: Royal Scottish Museum, 1954).

SAINT-AUBIN, Charles G de: *Art of the Embroiderer*, translated by Nikki Scheuer (Los Angeles: Los Angeles County Museum, 1983).

SCOTTISH ARTS COUNCIL: *Master Weavers: Tapestry from the Dovecot Studios 1912-1980* (Edinburgh: Canongate, 1980).

SCOTTISH DEVELOPMENT AGENCY: *Scottish Crafts Collection* (Edinburgh: Scottish Development Agency, c.1987).

SCOTT-MONCRIEFF, R: 'Notes on three Tapestry Hangings inventoried among the belongings of Mary of Guise, Queen Regent, and of her daughter, Mary Queen of Scots' in *Proceedings of the Society of Antiquaries of Scotland*, LI (1916-7), pp 108-16.

SCOTT-MONCRIEFF, R: 'Notes on some Sixteenth-Century Needle-work hangings in Dalmahoy House, and in the Royal Scottish Museum' in *Proceedings of the Society of Antiquaries of Scotland*, LII (1917-8), pp 72-81.

SEDGWICK, Romney (editor): *History of Parliament: The House of Commons 1715-1754* (Members E-Y) (London, 1970), volume II (Members E-Y).

SELIGMAN, G S and T Hughes: *Domestic Needlework: Its Origins and Customs throughout the Centuries* (London: *Country Life*, 1926).

SHERRILL, Sarah B: *Carpets and Rugs of Europe and America* (New York: Abbeville Press, 1996).

SLADE, Harry Gordon: *Glamis Castle* (London: The Society of Antiquaries of London, 2000).

STANILAND, Kay: *Medieval Craftsmen: Embroiderers* (London: British Museum Press, 1991).

STARKEY, David (editor): *The Inventory of King Henry VIII: The Transcript* (London: Harvey Miller Publishers, 1998).

STEVENSON, R K B: 'The Museum, its Beginnings and its Development': Part I 'to 1858', pp 31-85; Part II 'The National Museum to 1954', pp 142-211 in A S Bell (editor): *The Scottish Antiquarian Tradition: Essays to mark the bicentenary of the Society of Antiquaries of Scotland, 1780-1980* (Edinburgh: John Donald, 1981).

SWAIN, Margaret: *Historical Needlework: A study of influences in Scotland and Northern England* (London: Barrie & Jenkins, 1970).

SWAIN, Margaret: *The Needlework of Mary, Queen of Scots* (New York: Van Nostrand Reinhold, 1973).

SWAIN, Margaret: *Figures on Fabric: Embroidery designs and their application* (London: A & C Black, 1980).

SWAIN, Margaret: *Scottish Embroidery: Medieval to Modern* (London: B T Batsford, 1986).

SWAIN, Margaret: 'The Lochleven and Linlithgow Hangings' in *Proceedings of the Society of Antiquaries of Scotland*, 124 (1994), pp 455-66.

SYMONDS, Mary and Louisa Preece: *Needlework through the Ages* (London: Hodder & Stoughton, 1928).

TARRANT, Naomi E A: *Samplers in the Royal Scottish Museum* (Edinburgh: Royal Scottish Museum, 1978).

TARRANT, Naomi E A: 'The Bedroom' in *The Scottish Home*, edited by Annette Carruthers (Edinburgh: NMS Publishing, 1996).

TARRANT, Naomi E A: *Going to Bed* (Edinburgh: NMS Publishing, 1998).

TARRANT, Naomi E A: 'Scottish Linen Damasks of the Eighteenth Century' in *Riggisberger Berichte*, 7 (1999), pp 83-97.

TARRANT, Naomi E A: 'Textiles in the Home' in *Caring for the Scottish Home*, edited by Ian Davidson (Edinburgh: NMS Publishing and the National Trust for Scotland, 2001).

TAYLER, Henrietta: *History of the Family of Urquhart* (Aberdeen: The University Press, 1946).

TAYLOR, Roderick: *Embroidery of the Greek Islands* (Yeovil: Marston House/Taylor Kerwin Ltd, 1998).

THOMAS, Mary: *Mary Thomas's Dictionary of Embroidery Stitches* (London: Hodder & Stoughton, 1934).

WARDLE, Patricia: Guide to English Embroidery (London: HMSO, 1970).

WARDLE, Patricia: 'The King's Embroiderer: Edmund Harrison (1590-1667)': (1) 'The man and his milieu' in *Textile History*, 25 (1994), pp 29-59; (2) 'His Work' in *Textile History*, 26, 1995, pp 139-84

WATERSTON, Charles D: *Collections in Context: The Museum of the Royal Society of Edinburgh and the inception of a National Museum for Scotland* (Edinburgh: NMS Publishing, 1997).

WEAVERS WORKSHOP: *Weavers Workshop Newsletter* (Edinburgh: 1972-5).

WELLS-COLE, Anthony: *Art and Decoration in Elizabethan and Jacobean England: the influence of continental prints, 1558-1625* (London: Yale University Press, 1997).

WRIGHT, Isabella Murray: *Stirling Letters* (Stirling: Smith Art Gallery & Museum, 1998).

GLOSSARY

APPLIQUÉ: embroidery term for fabric cut out and sewn to a ground fabric, often with decorative stitches.

CARTOUCHE: an ornate frame, usually with scroll-like outline.

COCHINEAL: dye made from the bodies of female insects, *Dactylopius coccu.*

CONFRATERNITY: a religious or charitable brotherhood.

COPE: an ecclesiastical vestment, usually half a circle, worn over the shoulders, with a mock hood at the back.

CORDELIERE: a knotted cord worn by a Franciscan friar round his waist.

COUCHED-WORK: an embroidery term, threads that lie on the surface of the fabric and are held down by another thread going through to the back.

CUT-WORK: embroidery where part of the ground fabric has been cut away.

DAMASK: self patterned fabric, with a reversible design using a satin weave, the play of light showing the design in the contrast between the two faces of the weave.

DYER'S GREENWOOD: dye plant, *Genista tinctoria*, a form of broom.

FIGURED: design on fabric that contains figures, flowers or heraldic devices as opposed to geometric patterns.

FRENCH KNOT: an embroidery stitch made by twisting the thread two or three times round the needle before inserting it back into the fabric.

FUSTIAN: a fabric term which has changed its meaning over the centuries. Here it is used to describe a mixed cotton and linen fabric usually with a twill weave, used for large embroidered wall hangings and curtains in the 17th and 18th centuries.

GLITSAUMER: the Icelandic term for the embroidery technique of counted thread work.

GORES: inserts, usually triangular, to extend the width of a garment at the hem.

GUILLOCHE: term used for ornament imitating braided ribbonwork.

HOLBEIN STITCH: simple running stitch worked in both directions to create a continuous line. Also known as double running stitch.

IKAT: term used to describe a technique of dyeing the warp threads before weaving. Also known as chiné in Europe.

INDIGOTIN: the insoluble blue dye produced from woad or indigo plants.

GENISTEIN: weak yellowing colouring agent derived from dyer's greenwood.

KERMES: a red dye made from the dried bodies of female bugs *Kermes ilicis.*

LAC: a red dye made from the bodies of insects, *Laccifer lacca*, from Asia.

LUTEOLIN: yellowing colour agent derived from dyer's greenwood.

MADDER: dye made from the roots of the madder plant.

MICA: a silicate mineral with layered structure that produces small clear thin sheets, often used to imitate windows in embroideries in the 17th century.

NEEDLELACE: lace made with a continuous thread and a needle, as opposed to bobbin lace, a modified weaving technique, made from many threads, each wound round a bobbin, which are interwoven on a pillow to form the fabric.

OGEE: an S-shaped line.

OGIVAL: like a pointed or Gothic arch.

OLD FUSTIC: a yellow dye obtained from a tropical tree *Chlorophora tinctoria.*

OR NUÉ: an embroidery technique where gold or silver threads are laid on the fabric and then couched down using coloured silk threads to create the shading.

ORPHREYS: ornamental borders, usually embroidered, on ecclesiastical vestments.

PALAMPORE: a Hindi and Persian term meaning a bed-cover

PETIT POINT: an embroidery stitch, a slanted stitch, half of a cross-stitch.

RAISED WORK: parts of an embroidery, which has been raised up from the rest by padding, or by needlelace stitches.

ROCOCO STITCH: embroidery stitch worked on an even-weave canvas that looks like little bundles tied together when finished.

SELVAGE or SELVEDGE: the side edges of a woven cloth which help to strengthen it and keep the tension.

SPECKLING: embroidery stitch producing a speckled effect.

SUITES: a set of things, *eg* matching table cloth and napkins.

TAMBOURED: embroidery term used to refer to a technique where the stitches are worked from the back, using a small hook with the thread held taut in one hand on the front. The hook is inserted to pull the thread through to the other side. The stitch when finished resembles chain stitch. The term tambour, actually refers to a round frame used to hold the fabric taut whilst it is embroidered.

THIN LAYER CHROMATOGRAPHY: a technique for separating dissolved chemical substances through the use of glass plates coated with a thin layer of a finely ground absorbent such as silica gel. Useful for separating compounds of naturally occurring substances.

VISIBLE SPECTROPHOTOMETRY: a technique for measuring light in the visible spectrum wavelength by wavelength and used for measuring the reflection or transmission characteristics of coloured materials.

INDEX

[Illustrations denoted by italicised and underlined numbers]